M000223026

THE FOUR FACES OF GOD

'In this exciting book Tim Pain and the late John Bickersteth not only reveal love of the deep mysterious themes and connections of the four Gospels, they also reveal the qualities of a Christian who would follow the Master through his word. Here are warm, compelling and fresh insights into the truths of salvation. The combination of the old and the wise with the fresh and the younger is a splendid and helpful one.'

PETER BALL
Bishop of Gloucester

'John Bickersteth felt deeply and shared widely the views expressed in this book. I am delighted that a wider audience will now be able to share in this deep and vital teaching.'

MICHAEL HARPER

'John Bickersteth was a man faithful to God and to others. He loved his God, his family and the people of God. His life was truly an inspiration.'

LOREN CUNNINGHAM
President, Youth With A Mission

'John was always worth hearing; he listened, he loved, he lived as one of God's friends.'

MICHAEL BAUGHEN
Bishop of Chester

The Four Faces of God

JOHN BICKERSTETH & TIMOTHY PAIN

KINGSWAY PUBLICATIONS
EASTBOURNE

Copyright © Timothy Pain and
the Trustees of the Ashburnham Thanksgiving Trust 1992.
The right of Timothy Pain and the Trustees of the
Ashburnham Thanksgiving Trust to be identified
as authors of this work has been asserted by them in
accordance with the Copyright, Design
and Patents Act 1988.

First published 1992
Reprinted 1993, 1994

All rights reserved.
No part of this publication may be reproduced or
transmitted in any form or by any means, electronic
or mechanical, including photocopy, recording, or any
information storage and retrieval system, without
permission in writing from the publisher.

Unless otherwise indicated, biblical quotations are from the
New Jerusalem Bible © Darton, Longman and Todd Ltd
and Doubleday and Co Inc 1985

ISBN 0 85476 326 0

Produced by Bookprint Creative Services,
P.O. Box 827, BN21 3YJ, England for
KINGSWAY PUBLICATIONS LTD
Lottbridge Drove, Eastbourne, E. Sussex BN23 6NT.
Printed in Great Britain

Contents

Author's Note

I was first introduced to John Bickersteth back in April 1977. It was only a casual exchange of greetings at a public meeting, but John stood out in my memory: partly because he was surrounded by ladies dressed in purple, and partly because he was the first Old Etonian—and the first Anglican vicar—that I had met. He was tall and thin and he reminded me of my austere grammar school headmaster.

I met John for the second time the following February when I had settled in East Sussex and was visiting the local clergy to introduce myself and the work I hoped to do among young people. By then, colleagues had told me about John's near blindness, his remarkable inheritance, and his stature as the pioneer of charismatic renewal in Sussex. His local reputation awed me, as did the long, winding drive down into his stately home, but John soon put me at ease.

I introduced myself and was very flattered when he commented, 'My, God really is assembling his team.' But the link between us was forged when we realised that God had guided us through identical passages of Scripture into similar concerns and aims.

There was a cultural gulf between us, which often surfaced in the years that followed. John was nearly thirty years my senior. He was an aristocrat; I was from a council house. He was a gentleman; I was more rough hewn. He was an Anglican; I had been raised to believe that real Christians went to Baptist churches. He was from Sussex; I was from South London. Yet both of us were convinced that God's essential directive to us as individuals lay in the Old Testament references to restoring ruined cities and rebuilding ancient walls.

In particular, we discovered that Isaiah 58:10–12 was the key passage which God was using to direct our different work in rural East Sussex: for me it was still only a vision, whereas John had been working it out for almost twenty years. I left the meeting convinced that I had been listening to an apostle.

It was another month before I first heard John preach, and his sermon changed my life. It was John's standard introduction to the fourfold principle, but the concept and ideas were new to me. They set me thinking and reading the New Testament as nothing had before.

After almost five years of youth evangelism, at John's invitation I moved to Ashburnham Place (the Christian conference centre which is based at John's ancestral home) to join the small residential community which was living in a rebuilt stable and was working and praying for renewal and unity among East Sussex churches. It was an opportunity to study, pray, discuss, argue and disagree with John and others; and there followed five years of experimentation, frustration, excitement, despair and laughter. Although the community focused on charismatic issues, John's fourfold ideas were always in the background: shaping, testing and directing everything that we did.

Some people became bored with John's apparent obsession with the fourfold principle. But the more I researched, studied and tested his ideas, the more I became convinced that they were needed to help restore the church to balanced, healthy and fruitful Christianity.

It is almost impossible for me to overstate the importance of this fourfold understanding of God and the gospel. It is not a set of clever ideas about Jesus. It is not an alternative way of handling the four Gospels. It is not a human device which has to be applied to everything in Christianity. It is nothing to do with the number four. And it is not even a new idea, for it dates from the first five centuries. But it is spiritual dynamite. For me and many others in

East Sussex, our fourfold understanding has transformed the way we worship, evangelise, pray, preach, use charismatic ministries, and—most importantly—relate with Christians from other traditions. The principle behind our understanding of the four faces of God doesn't look much on paper, but it certainly packs a punch.

Cancer forced John to retire in 1988, and doctors gave him a very short life expectancy. But as John was still alive in late 1990, and looked as though he might live on for several years, a few of us encouraged him to start writing this book.

Early in October 1991, John's wife delivered a package to my door: John wanted my opinion on what he had written. For some reason that I cannot explain, instead of putting it in my in-tray, I started work on it straightaway. I was thrilled with what he had managed to write, but it was far from complete, and it wasn't John at his best. The following day I sent John my initial response, outlining four main worries about the manuscript. Minutes after I had posted my critical letter, the telephone rang: John's kidneys had unexpectedly failed during his thirty-first course of chemotherapy, and the doctors said that he had only hours to live. How I wished that I could recover my letter from the post office!

In fact, John lived on for another week and spent some of that time discussing, and laughing about, my letter. He knew then that he would never complete the book, so he repeated the request, first made many months earlier, that I finish it for him.

I was torn between maintaining what John had written as a memorial to one of God's spiritual giants, and crafting the best possible book, using old tapes and notes, as well as John's draft manuscript. I discussed it with my editor, and with John's wife and children, and we all agreed that I should thoroughly reshape John's manuscript and also add what was missing.

Co-writing this book with a man in paradise has been extremely difficult: time and again I would have given anything to ask John some questions! I can't write like an Old Etonian, so most of the words that follow are mine. But, equally, most of the ideas are John's. We discussed all of the material many times in the fourteen years that we knew each other and eventually reached similar conclusions. Some sections contain ideas which I developed too recently for them to have been revised by John. I hope that he agrees with me!

Whenever John gave an introductory talk about the fourfold principle, characteristically, he always began by understating his feelings for the material. He usually started with these words:

> My study of this subject has been of tremendous help to my Christian life, in deepening my love for Christ, and in understanding who he is and what he really came to do. I trust that what has been such a blessing to me may prove of some help to those present today.

The ideas expressed in this book shaped a man who, in the judgement of those who felt his influence, was one of the most remarkable British Christian leaders of the twentieth century. They have helped me greatly. I hope that they may help you too.

Timothy Pain
1992

With gratitude to all those people whose prayers, patience, and perceptive comments through the last thirty years have helped to shape this book.

Especially: the staff at Ashburnham Place
            the members of the Stable Family
            the congregations in Ashburnham and Penhurst
            and John's wife Marlis, and his three children,
            Richard, Bob and Caroline

Introduction

In this book we seek to show what John Bickersteth has called 'the fourfold principle'. This is our belief that it has pleased the Holy Spirit to reveal the essence of God's nature in four main aspects or faces: as powerful king, suffering servant, perfect human being and holy God.

God's nature is rich and complex, and obviously he reveals himself in a vast number of different ways. John recognised this, but maintained that four primary aspects of God's nature predominate. The book is not an exhaustive examination of all the ways God has revealed himself, but focuses on these four main characteristics.

The four faces of God may be seen throughout Scripture: in different parts of the Old Testament; in the four Gospels, where they are starkly evident in the life and ministry of Jesus; and in the Acts, Epistles and Revelation. Moreover—I will argue—they should be held in balance and revealed in the lives of all Christians and the church.

John Bickersteth's thesis was that there are four Gospels precisely because God has four main aspects. He maintained that each Gospel emphasises a different aspect of God. Obviously all the faces can be seen in all the Gospels, as can other aspects of God's nature, but John argued that when we look at the differences between the Gospels we see four different emphases.

This book does not pretend to give a detailed study of the four Gospels. Rather, it attempts to highlight the differences between the Gospels in order to show that, in general, these differences portray Jesus from four viewpoints. In Part One I will suggest that the kingly face can be seen more clearly in Matthew, the serving face in Mark, the perfect humanity of Jesus in Luke, and his divine holiness in John. But nothing I write should be taken to suggest that only one face can be seen in each Gospel.

Over twenty-five years ago, John devised some diagrams which helped him to teach this fourfold principle. After much agonising, I have thoroughly revised his diagrams and my amended diagrams appear throughout this book. In Part One I build up the diagrams, seeking to arouse a sense of anticipation, and to allow space for some creative thinking by readers. In these chapters I highlight some of the characteristic differences between the Gospels, so the four Gospels are in the same position in each diagram—John is always at the top, for example.

In Part Two I look beyond the Gospels, and take as my starting point the four main aspects of God. In this second half of the book, the four sides of each diagram represent the four faces of God. Now each aspect is in the same position in all the diagrams—the serving face is always at the bottom, for example.

By their nature, the diagrams over-simplify the argument. Seen on their own, they can suggest a rigid understanding which has no room for flexibility, exceptions or overlap. Yet when they are read in conjunction with the text, it should be clear that this is not what I suggest. I hope the diagrams enhance the book and I trust that readers will grasp my oft-repeated point that I am describing a general principle, not a fixed rule.

In Part Two I introduce a series of 'foursomes' which illustrate and apply the fourfold principle. Some of these are self-evident; others are convincing; most require some thought and study; one or two stretch the principle to make a small point!

A preacher can, by means of a twinkle in the eye, a shrug or smile, show his or her congregation that a particular remark is made 'tongue in cheek'. John always offered a few foursomes in this way. I have preserved them as interesting, even provocative, observations, but they are not vital to the argument.

I am sure that most readers will want to reject or vary some of the foursomes: although John and I agreed on the general principle, we disagreed about some of the fine detail. At times we could both see four clear points, yet could not agree on how they corresponded with the four aspects of God. I have changed two of John's classifications, and would have liked to have changed two more!

Wherever possible, I have tried to avoid technical terms. I have not used words like 'redaction' or 'synoptic', and have not referred to Q or S or Christology. However, some terms do not have meaningful alternatives.

Virtually all Bible teachers agree that the Gospels are both inspired and authoritative, but they go on to disagree about the character of this inspiration and authority. Whenever I suggest that the fourfold principle is inspired, I do not have a particular theory of inspiration in mind, for it is another area where John and I disagreed. It is a little like our views on creation. We agreed that God created the world, but we could not agree on how he had done it, what means he had used, and how long it had taken him. I hope that this book will stimulate all readers, whatever their beliefs about inspiration.

Like so many today, in our approach to the Gospels John and I fall between the fundamental and the liberal camps. We both hold the sort of views which cause many liberals to charge us with fundamentalism, and most fundamentalists to classify us as liberals!

In Part One I focus entirely on the differences between the Gospels. John and I could not agree with those who suggest that every discrepancy can be explained, nor with those who think that the differences threaten their faith. Scholars have produced many plausible theories about the differences, but our work does not depend on any one theory, nor does it offer itself as an alternative theory. We do not ask or answer the question: 'How did the differences between the Gospels arise?' Instead we ask: 'What can we learn about God from the differences between the Gospels?' And it is these differences that have greatly enhanced our understanding of God, our devotion to Jesus, and our appreciation of Christian unity. As a result we want to stand with, and learn from, all those Christians who hold different views from ourselves about the Gospels.

I thank all those people who have read the many versions of this manuscript and have offered such helpful critical comments and advice, all those who have offered encouragement and support, all those who have prayed for its completion and publication, and all those who have helped in some practical way—especially Caroline Bickersteth, Andrew and Sandra Budd, Catherine Butcher, Jane Collins, Winifred Cox, Vivien Culver, Peter Dann, Stuart Davison, David and Christine Freeland, Geoff and Katie Gray, Richard Herkes, Sue Lindsay, Richard Martin, Ian and Lucinda McNaughton, Michael and Jennifer Oldroyd, Alan Pain, Alison Pain, Edith Pain, Liz Pearman, Rhona Pipe, Geoff and Sheila Ridsdale, Tommy Tucker, and Michael and Gillian Warren.

I offer this book on John's behalf in the hope that it will stimulate our readers to study the Scriptures more deeply, to serve other people more sacrificially, to identify more closely with Christians of different traditions, and to worship their heavenly Father more creatively.

Timothy Pain

If you want to get the most out of this book, turn now to page 88 and attempt question 1—in pencil—before reading Part One. Do not check your answers!

When you complete the exercise *after* reading Part One, you will find out how much the book has helped you.

PART ONE

1

Four Different Gospels

Everybody knows that there are four accounts of the life and death of Jesus Christ in the New Testament. But few people go on to ask why there are four accounts and not six, for example, or three or just one. Most people assume that the number must be some sort of accident.

Again, everybody knows that these four accounts present some events differently, and at times even appear to conflict with each other. But few people ask themselves why God has allowed these differences to exist. Some gloss over them as embarrassing mysteries, others see them as evidence that the witnesses were fallible, while a third group believes them to be proof that the Bible is more fiction than fact.

But those Christians who believe that the Gospels are the perfect work of God the Holy Spirit in portraying the Person and work of Jesus should surely expect, first, that the number of Gospels is not accidental but vital to a right understanding of Jesus, and, second, that any differences between the Gospels will be God-breathed and useful for refuting error, for guiding people's lives and for teaching on uprightness.

This book is an attempt to answer these two apparently insignificant questions. It tries to explain why there are four New Testament accounts of Jesus' life and why the differences between the four accounts are so important. The answers to these two questions will shed light on almost every facet of the Christian life.

Writing down the Gospels

In the first century after Christ's resurrection, many men of widely different backgrounds and experiences wrote down the story of Jesus as they understood it, basing their work on their own memory, on oral traditions, on other people's written records and—in some cases—on imagination.

The documents now called Matthew, Mark, Luke and John were not the only accounts of Jesus' life to circulate among early believers, but they were always pre-eminent. Scholars believe that there was a gap of about one generation between the resurrection of Jesus and the writing of the first Gospel, and that most of Paul's letters were written before the four Gospels. John was the last of the four Gospels to be written and within a few decades of its publication an unknown Christian had gathered the four together and begun circulating them as one collection of four Gospels. By AD 150 these four Gospels had been generally accepted as authoritative records of Christ's life and death but it was another hundred years before they were widely recognised as the only authoritative accounts.

Towards the end of the second century, churches in different parts of the world began to gather together the writings of the first-century Christians. A Gospel or letter was recognised as Holy Scripture when there was good evidence that it was written by an apostle or by a member of the apostolic circle. At first, there was a great deal of disagreement about some of the letters, especially James, Hebrews and Revelation, but there was complete unanimity about Matthew, Mark and Luke, and general agreement about John.

During the third century, Eusebius, one of the Fathers of the early church, summarised Christian opinion at the time by dividing books into three categories: those that were 'spurious', those that were 'disputed', and those that were 'acknowledged'. The acknowledged books were the four Gospels, Acts, 1 Peter, 1 John and Paul's letters.

The New Testament was finally fixed in AD 367 by the Eastern Church, in Athanasius' thirty-ninth Paschal letter; and in AD 397 by the Western Church, at the Council of Carthage. Both churches agreed that the twenty-seven books known today as the New Testament should be accepted as God-breathed Scripture.

In the sixteenth century, the Roman and the Protestant Churches both debated the validity of some of the New Testament books, but not the four Gospels. (Both churches eventually reaffirmed their adherence to the traditional twenty-seven books of the New Testament.)

Debating the differences

During the twentieth century, theological debate has not centred on the legitimacy of particular New Testament books, but on the value, the inspiration, the accuracy and the authority of all the New Testament books, and especially of the four Gospels. As a result of widespread disagreement about the character of the Gospels' authority, Christians who profess to believe in their full inspiration and absolute authority have often glossed over the differences between the four—and have even tried to pretend that differences do not exist. In an attempt to defend the single authorship of the Holy Spirit working through men, some Christians have mistakenly suggested that each account must be trying to say the same thing.

Other Christians have been so aware of the difficulties of harmonising the four Gospels that at times they have appeared to reject the concept of divine authority and to forget that all Scripture is inspired by God.

In this book, as we have said, we maintain that the Gospels do sometimes present the same incident in different ways, but these differences do not invalidate Scripture and need not embarrass believers. Christians have recognised the problem of the discrepancies between the Gospels since the earliest days of the church. Marcion, the second-century church leader whom some consider to have been heretical, tried to solve the problem of the differences by using only his own amended version of Luke. Ever since, there have been innumerable attempts to produce one Gospel which includes and harmonises all the details from the four,

and which sets out the events of Jesus' life in the order they sup-
posedly took place.

Many of these attempts have been based on the idea that the
four Gospels merely supplement or corroborate each other. But
we believe that the Gospels are much more than repetitive tes-
timonies. Instead, each Gospel has its own distinctive object, each
makes its own selection and arrangement of facts, and each stresses different aspects of the rich tradition of the message of Jesus.
The differences between the four Gospels, far from being embarrassing, need to be recognised as vital to the revelation of Jesus
and to be valued as important elements of the good news.

It is for this reason that any harmony of the Gospels, or of any
part of the Gospels, though interesting, detracts from God's purpose in presenting the gospel story in four ways. When we arrange
the events in a supposed chronological order, we take them out of
the passages in which they appear in each Gospel. As a result, they
lose the force they possess when they are read in their original
context. The facts about Jesus are important however they are
read and received, but they are twice as meaningful when we
understand why each writer has included them in a particular
sequence of events.

The first three Gospels

The problem of the differences between the Gospels is most acute
with the first three Gospels, and nobody can know for certain
how and when they were written. It is possible to believe that they
were written in their present form by Matthew, Mark and Luke.
It is also possible to accept them as authoritative books, fully
inspired by God, without accepting that their traditionally designated authors were primarily responsible for them. And it is also
possible to believe that the original documents were edited several
times by a team of first-century editors who themselves were fully
inspired by God as they worked on the material. If we probe the
Gospels to find out how they were assembled it does not necessarily mean that we doubt their divine inspiration.

It is not disputed that the apostles passed on orally those details of Jesus' life and death that they themselves had witnessed. And it is obvious that this oral tradition had to be written down when the eye-witnesses began to die or disperse. Different collections of Jesus' deeds and words would then have been circulated. It is surely likely that the Gospel writers selected material from these diverse collections when they assembled their Gospels.

Tradition asserts that Matthew's Gospel was the first to be written, but since the nineteenth century most Protestant scholars have believed that Mark was the first Gospel, though a few have recently returned to the more traditional view.

The authors and editors of the Gospels, whoever they were, for the Gospels were all written anonymously, appear to have used some of the same sources as well as their own independent sources. And the authors of Matthew and Luke certainly seem at some stage to have used early drafts of Mark's Gospel.

As with any book or literary project, it is likely that there was a lengthy process of prayer, reading, research, consultation, listening, writing, rewriting, checking, revision and editing. This process was guided by the Holy Spirit who motivated people to write and helped them to preserve, select and arrange their material.

The writers were real people. Each had a different background, special interests, varied literary abilities and contrasting theological emphases. The Holy Spirit did not override the authors' gifts and interests; instead, he used and enhanced them, enabling each of them to craft a Gospel that presents a different view of Jesus' Person and mission.

Appreciating the differences

Not many believers today know that the Gospels give Jesus different titles. Fewer still know why they do this. Most believers know that Matthew and Luke record different versions of Jesus' birth, but most have not been taught why Luke leaves out the Wise Men, or why Matthew focuses on Joseph, or why Mark and John begin as they do. Each Christmas, in churches throughout the land, a homogenised version of the nativity story is told which thwarts God's purpose in causing the story to be written in four quite different ways.

Some believers know which Gospel contains the story of the good Samaritan, and which one records the story of the workers in the vineyard; but few grasp why they are in those Gospels and why this is so important. Nearly all believers know that the four Gospels record seven sayings of Christ on the cross; but hardly any know that the words 'Father, forgive' are only mentioned in one Gospel—and can state which one and why. Everybody knows that Jesus washed his disciples' feet before the Last Supper, but how many realise what the story teaches by virtue of being recorded in John?

There are hundreds of differences between the Gospels. It is likely that Jesus used the same stories and sermons many times, with inevitable small variations in detail. Any writer who knew more than one version of a sermon or parable would surely have used whichever variant was most relevant to his viewpoint. Each writer also included material which is unique to his Gospel. And they all appear to have ignored some incidents, examples and details that they knew about. This was all done under the guidance of God's Holy Spirit.

Four different Gospels

Looking at the Gospels is rather like looking at a mountain from the four points of the compass. The aspects are entirely different, though it is the same mountain. A traveller familiar with the mountain only from the north, for example, might be shown a photograph of the mountain from the south and vehemently deny that it is the same mountain.

Or it is as if a bottle of wine and a vase of flowers were placed next to each other on a table. A man on one side of the table would swear that the wine was to the right of the vase, but a woman opposite him would insist that they were the other way around. A man on the third side would be sure that the wine was behind the vase, and the woman opposite him would disagree. Similarly, in the Gospels the same event may be recorded differently because it is seen from different viewpoints.

The differences between the four Gospels do not exist to confuse people; they are there because there are four main ways of looking at Jesus. And in the next four chapters of this book we will try to describe these ways and to show that Jesus reveals the four main faces of God. We will then go on from these viewpoints to suggest that humankind has four main needs, and that Jesus has four great relationships with men and women; that there were four main reasons why Jesus came, and four types of miracle during his life; that there were four primary reasons for his death, and four blessings for his disciples; that there are four important responses for the church today, and four basic messages which must be proclaimed to the world; and that there are many more 'foursomes' which are valuable for study, mission, worship and balanced Christian discipleship.

2

Matthew's View of Jesus

Matthew's differences suggest that he views Jesus as a king who has come to found a kingdom. Throughout his Gospel he highlights issues of leadership and authority and focuses on God's heavenly kingdom.

In his first verse Matthew describes Jesus Christ as the 'son of David, son of Abraham'. By linking Jesus with Abraham, the father and founder of the nation, and with David, Israel's greatest king, Matthew teaches that Jesus is the heir of Abraham's Genesis 17 covenant and that he is great David's greater son, in whom the promises given to David will be fulfilled.

The genealogy (1:1–17)

Matthew establishes Jesus' royal credentials by placing a genealogy at the start of the Gospel. He traces Jesus' descent down from Abraham, through David and the line of Israel's kings, to Joseph, Jesus' official father.

Matthew, who elsewhere pays little attention to women, mentions four in his genealogy. He ignores obvious female ancestors like Sarah and Rebekah, and points instead to a mother by incest, a prostitute, a foreigner and an adulteress (Tamar, Rahab, Ruth and Bathsheba). The first three were Gentiles, and all four changed the blood line of the covenant family. They prepare Matthew's readers for another change in the kingdom and for the wholesale integration of Gentiles into God's family.

The nativity (1:18–2:23)

Matthew includes unique material in his account of the nativity. His version underlines the theme of authority, illustrates Jesus' kingship and sheds light on the mystery of God's developing kingdom. The action centres on Joseph (the head of the household) and stresses his perfect obedience; Mary is hardly mentioned. God speaks to Joseph in dreams, revealing his plan to save his people. And Matthew comments that these events fulfil God's promises to the prophets—a point he returns to throughout his Gospel.

Jesus is called 'Immanuel' (1:23)—God-is-with-us—a name which shows that God does not forsake his people. Bethlehem is identified as the promised location from which a leader will come to rule God's people (2:5–6). Great men of the east, recognised by tradition as kings, enquire, 'Where is the infant king of the Jews?' (2:2). The news of a royal birth alarms the Jewish king Herod and perturbs all Jerusalem but thrills the wise Gentiles who offer the child gifts fit for a king.

The nativity

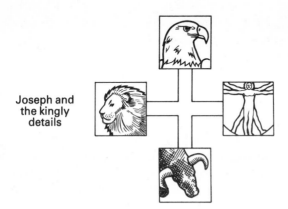

Joseph and
the kingly
details

Matthew portrays the nativity as a conflict between kings and alternative ways of ruling. The jealous and powerful usurper, Herod, misuses his authority, attempts to deceive the Wise Men, tries to kill Jesus and massacres the young boys of Bethlehem. The rightful heir is peaceful, vulnerable, gentle; and he is protected by God, who works through obedient men. By the end of chapter 2, Herod is dead, whereas Jesus is safe in Nazareth.

John the Baptist (3:1–17)

The kingdom of heaven is introduced in chapter 3. Matthew records John preaching, 'Repent, for the kingdom of Heaven is close at hand' (3:2); while Mark and Luke state that he preaches 'a baptism of repentance for the forgiveness of sins': in substance the same as Matthew, but phrased in a way which suits their different views. All three writers quote from Isaiah 40, but Matthew records only the authoritative command, 'Prepare a way for the Lord, make his paths straight' (3:3), while Mark and Luke extend the quotation in different ways, which suit their viewpoints.

Matthew continues, 'His winnowing-fan is in his hand; he will clear his threshing-floor and gather his wheat into his barn; but the chaff he will burn in a fire that will never go out' (3:12): language which is perfectly appropriate for the Lord of the kingdom. These words are not included by Mark and are inappropriate to his portrayal of Christ.

Only Matthew records John's recognition of Jesus' authority, expressed in his reluctance to baptise Jesus: 'It is I who need baptism from you' (3:14). And when the voice speaks from heaven, in Mark and Luke it reassures Jesus, with 'You are my Son,' but in Matthew it proclaims to everybody, 'This is my Son' (3:17).

Jesus was only baptised once, but the Holy Spirit inspired the writers to record the event from four different viewpoints. Matthew's small variations underscore Jesus' authority. In a harmonised account these are either overlooked (as with Matthew's recording of 'This is') or over-emphasised (as with Matthew's account of John's reluctance).

The temptations (4:1–25)

John ignores Jesus' temptations. Mark only mentions them briefly. Matthew and Luke tell similar stories but with significant differences. Matthew implies that the devil comes to Jesus with three temptations only after Jesus has been weakened by fasting for forty days and nights. He suggests that the climax of the temptations is the devil's offer to give Jesus all the kingdoms of the world. And he states that when Jesus has overcome these temptations, angels appear and look after him. These touches can be especially appreciated by those who are looking for a king.

After mentioning John's arrest, Matthew gives his fifth example of the way Jesus fulfilled the purposes of God foretold by the prophets (4:15–16) and describes Jesus' essential message as, 'Repent, for the kingdom of Heaven is close at hand' (4:17).

The Sermon on the Mount (5:1–7:29)

Chapters 5–7 are even more distinctive to Matthew and are the first of Matthew's five blocks of teaching (5–7; 10; 13; 18; 24–25). Matthew's use of five blocks of teaching parallels the five books of the Pentateuch (Genesis to Deuteronomy) and suggests that Jesus is a second Moses, a second law-giver. This is entirely in keeping with Matthew's view of Jesus as an authoritative ruler.

In this first teaching section, which begins with a beatitude about the kingdom of heaven, Jesus authoritatively unfolds some principles of his kingdom and sets out the standards of behaviour he expects from his subjects. To underline their authority, some sayings are introduced with the solemn Hebrew word *Amen* ('verily' or 'in truth'); and this note of authority is enhanced by Jesus' repeated use of 'I tell you' or 'I say this to you'.

Matthew uses the word 'uprightness' (some translations have 'righteousness' or 'saving justice') several times in the Sermon. The other three writers use this word hardly at all but it appears time and again throughout Matthew's Gospel, along with the word 'the upright' or 'the righteous'. For example, while Luke refers to 'the blood of Abel' (Lk 11:51), Matthew has 'the blood of righteous Abel' (23:35, NIV) and whereas Luke writes, 'Set your hearts on his kingdom, and these other things will be given you as well' (Lk 12:31), Matthew writes, 'Set your hearts on his kingdom first, and on God's saving justice, and all these other things will be given you as well' (6:33). For Matthew, uprightness is a central characteristic of God's kingdom while other aspects are more important to Mark, Luke and John.

Key word

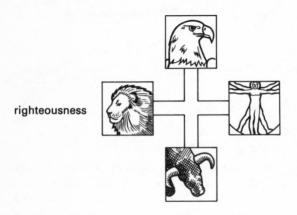

righteousness

Matthew emphasises that Jesus has not come to abolish the Law and the Prophets but to fulfil them by giving them a new and definitive form. He makes repeated references to the kingdom, whose character is implied in its distinctive title, 'the kingdom of heaven', a title which only appears in Matthew. His version of the Lord's Prayer differs from Luke's by the inclusion of the clause 'your will be done on earth as in heaven' (6:10). And Matthew closes the Sermon, first with Jesus' explanation that only those people who do the will of the Father in heaven will enter the kingdom of heaven, and then with the comment that Jesus made a deep impression on the people because he taught with authority.

Ten miracles (8:1–9:37)

After collecting together those sayings of Jesus which describe the heavenly character and moral authority of the kingdom (the Sermon on the Mount), Matthew gathers together ten miracles which illustrate the physical and spiritual authority of the kingdom. These miracles show Jesus as ruler over nature, ruler over diseases and ruler over devils. Lepers are healed, the dead are revived, devils fear, a storm obeys; but God's people of Israel will not receive their king.

Jesus' miracles show

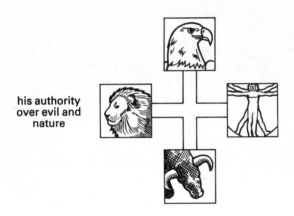

his authority over evil and nature

Many of the scenes in chapters 8–9 are also found in Mark and Luke, with characteristic differences which emphasise each writer's viewpoint. Only Matthew reports that in fulfilment of God's revealed purposes, 'He himself bore our sicknesses away and carried our diseases' (8:17). Only Matthew mentions Jesus' quotation from Hosea: 'Mercy is what pleases me' (9:13 [repeated again in Matthew 12:7]). And only Matthew writes, '. . . many will come from east and west and sit down with Abraham and

Isaac and Jacob at that feast in the kingdom of Heaven; but the children of the kingdom will be thrown into the darkness outside' (8:11–12). Israel will not have Jesus but he still goes on preaching 'the good news of the kingdom' (9:35) to crowds for whom he feels sorry because they are harassed and dejected, like sheep who do not have a shepherd to lead them.

Rejection and opposition (10:1–11:30)

In chapter 11, Matthew shows what Jesus is like under pressure. First, his witness, John the Baptist, doubts him. Then he compares the Jews to children whom it is impossible to please (11:16–19). Finally, the towns in which most of his miracles have been worked remain unchanged. Yet Matthew records Jesus responding to these disappointments, not with despair, but with these words: 'I bless you, Father, Lord of heaven and earth . . . Yes, Father, for that is what it pleased you to do' (11:25– 26).

The same words come in Luke's Gospel, but there they are a natural human response to the jubilation of the seventy-two (Lk 10:17–22). Matthew uses the words differently, to illustrate the king's meek character, and immediately follows them with words which only he reports:

Come to me, all you who labour and are overburdened, and I will give you rest. Shoulder my yoke and learn from me, for I am gentle and humble in heart, and you will find rest for your souls. Yes, my yoke is easy and my burden light (11:28–30).

Only a gentle leader, who can rejoice in rejection and offer thanks in disappointment, can give lasting rest and peace to his subjects.

Questions (12:1–50)

Most of the incidents related in chapter 12 are also found in Mark and Luke but Matthew adds some important phrases. In the cornfield, Jesus says, 'Have you not read in the Law that on the

Sabbath day the Temple priests break the Sabbath without committing any fault? Now here, I tell you, is something greater than the Temple' (12:5–6)—words suited by their authority to illustrate Matthew's viewpoint. Matthew explains Jesus' request for anonymity as another fulfilment of prophecy and he quotes Isaiah 42 to describe the gentle nature of the kingdom and its impact on Gentile nations.

When Matthew reports the people's reaction to the cure of a blind and dumb demoniac, his crowd asks, 'Can this be the son of David?' (12:23), whereas Luke's crowd are merely amazed. (In Luke, the demoniac is described only as dumb. Matthew often underlines Jesus' authority by listing several ailments or all the people healed, whereas Luke usually understates Jesus' power by mentioning only one ailment or one person helped.)

Then, when the Pharisees debate with Jesus about exorcism, Matthew records two sayings which are only appropriate to a king or judge: 'I tell you this, that for every unfounded word people utter they will answer on Judgement Day' (12:36); and, 'That is what will happen to this wicked generation' (12:45).

Special insights

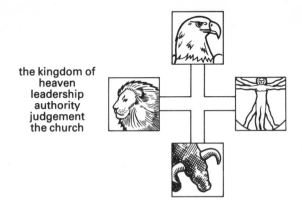

the kingdom of
heaven
leadership
authority
judgement
the church

Parables of the kingdom (13:1–52)

Next, Matthew tells seven parables to unfold 'the mysteries of the kingdom of Heaven' (13:11). Three are found in other Gospels but Matthew includes four of his own in a progression which moves from sowing, through growth, to harvest.

This series of parables suggests much about the value of the kingdom, the opposition to the kingdom, and the king's exclusive right to act as judge. Interspersed with the parables are more examples of the way Jesus fulfils God's purposes as revealed by the prophets.

Jesus' parables illustrate

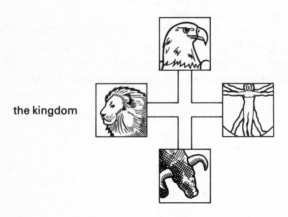

the kingdom

The church (13:53–18:35)

This central narrative section includes very little material which belongs only to Matthew. But Matthew adds some touches which underline his themes. He punctuates the section with three episodes featuring Peter, who was to become the first leader of the church. Peter's sinking is contrasted with Jesus' complete authority over the forces of nature. When the wind drops, the disciples bow down before Jesus (14:28–33). The Canaanite woman addresses Jesus as 'Lord, Son of David' (15:22). Jesus calls the Pharisees and Sadducees 'an evil and unfaithful generation' and tells them that they will be given the sign of Jonah (16:4). And Peter identifies Jesus at Caesarea Philippi, not only as 'the Christ' (the anointed man), but also as the Son of 'the living God' (16:16)—in the Old Testament, a title usually given to God when he works powerful miracles.

Matthew is the only Gospel writer to mention 'the church' (16:18) and he records Jesus' promise that it will be given royal power and heavenly authority: 'The gates of the underworld can never overpower it. I will give you the keys of the kingdom of Heaven' (16:18–19). This is followed by Jesus' transfiguration, which is prefaced in Matthew 16:28 by the suggestion that the display is a glimpse or sample of the coming kingdom. The exorcism of the epileptic demoniac comes next and Matthew explains that the disciples' failure of authority was due to lack of faith. Matthew goes on to record the miracle of the shekel in the fish's mouth. This miracle, which is only recorded by Matthew, demonstrates Jesus' faith and authority in the context of obedience to earthly rulers.

Then the disciples ask Jesus, 'Who is the greatest in the kingdom of Heaven?' (18:1). Jesus' answer in Matthew is, 'In truth I tell you, unless you change and become like little children you will never enter the kingdom of Heaven' (18:3); whereas Jesus' answer in Mark expresses a different but complementary truth: 'If anyone wants to be first, he must make himself last of all and servant of all' (Mk 9:35).

This section closes with a passage exclusive to Matthew (18:15–20), which again refers to the church and draws attention to its authority in judgement and in prayer, and with another parable about the kingdom of heaven (18:21–35, the unforgiving debtor), a parable to show that the kingdom is characterised by fair judgement.

The approaching kingdom (19:1–23:39)

Jesus' teaching is over for a while and he is on his way to Jerusalem. Once again, Matthew focuses attention on issues of authority and the kingdom of heaven. Much of the material in chapters 19–22 is mirrored in Mark and Luke, but Matthew does not include passages which are not relevant to his viewpoint and he includes others which are.

Only Matthew mentions: 'Eunuchs . . . who have made themselves so for the sake of the kingdom of Heaven' (19:12); the disciples sitting 'on twelve thrones to judge the twelve tribes of Israel' (19:28); a parable about the kingdom which describes a just and generous landowner (20:1–16); and a second blind man at Jericho (20:30). Matthew does not include the incident of the widow's mite, nor does he include most of the details in Mark which stress the place of serving (these will be examined in chapter 3). But 20:24–28 is exactly the same as Mark 10:41–45 and it directly relates to Matthew's theme of authority.

Jesus is

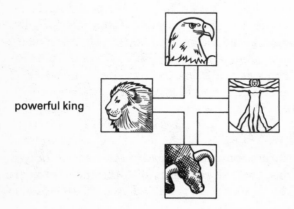

powerful king

It should not be surprising that Matthew reports Jesus' entry into Jerusalem as a king more fully than the other three Gospels. Typically, only he refers to two animals, thus showing Jesus' literal fulfilment of Zechariah's prophecy (21:1–5); only he reports Jesus' miracles in the Temple and children who shout out in the Temple, 'Hosanna to the son of David' (21:14–15); and only he records another parable about the kingdom of heaven, this time showing that the king can choose whom he likes to enter his kingdom (22:1–14).

Chapter 23 is almost entirely unique to Matthew: it is a sevenfold indictment of the way the scribes and the Pharisees abuse their authority, neglect the Law and do not behave uprightly. Only the kingly Jesus seen in Matthew speaks so fiercely and proclaims such a severe judgement.

The end and the second coming (24:1–25:46)

This is another section which is distinctive to Matthew: it is concerned with detailed teaching about the Second Coming of the king who will return with universal authority to judge and to rule. In chapter 24, as throughout his Gospel, Matthew draws together material which is scattered by Luke, offers it in more detail than Mark and includes small phrases which underline his view. He adds a question from the disciples about 'your coming' (24:3); states that the 'good news of the kingdom will be proclaimed' (24:14); and makes no mention of the Holy Spirit. He follows this with his last three parables which describe different facets of the final judgement and are only recorded by Matthew (chapter 25).

The passion and the resurrection (26:1–28:20)

In the main, Matthew's account of the passion and resurrection is the same as Mark's. Once again, it is in the differences between the Gospels that the writers' viewpoints are seen. Matthew goes into more detail than the others about Judas' betrayal of Jesus and is the only writer to record his suicide—it is Matthew's final example of a fulfilment of God's purposes revealed in advance by the prophets (27:3–10). He gives a very full account of Jesus' trial by the Roman governor, Pilate, and is the only writer to mention Pilate's wife's dream and Pilate's handwashing (27:19–24). Predictably, Matthew makes much of the Governor's question, 'Are you the king of the Jews?' (27:11) and of the soldiers' mocking cries: 'Hail, king of the Jews!' (27:29).

The passion emphasis

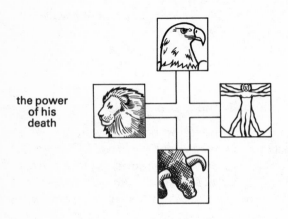

the power of his death

Matthew's differences underline the power of Jesus' death: only he records the supernatural earthquake (27:51), the opening of the tombs (27:52) and the appearance of resurrected holy people (27:52). And his exclusive material reinforces the supernatural power of Jesus' resurrection—the guards (27:62–65), the seals on the sepulchre stone (27:66), the violent earthquake (28:2) and the angel who rolls the stone away (28:2). Matthew mentions three further details which are not included in the other Gospels and are typical of his emphases: the women bow down before Jesus (28:9); the women obey Jesus (28:10–11); and the unrighteous Jewish authorities tell lies (28:11–15).

Matthew closes his Gospel by selecting these words from

among all those spoken by Jesus after his resurrection: 'All authority in heaven and on earth has been given to me' (28:18). The king reigns and he commands his subjects to teach others 'to observe all the commands I gave you' (28:20). And with those two notes of authority and obedience Matthew ends his account of the good news of Jesus the king.

The ending

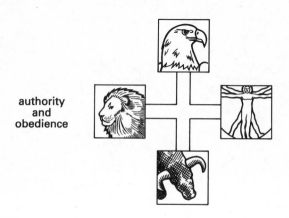

authority
and
obedience

Special insights

The Gospel according to Matthew was written from the kingdom point of view and focuses on the kingly face of God; the other three aspects can often be seen but the kingly emphasis predominates. Throughout this Gospel, Jesus' authority is emphasised—especially his power over evil and natural forces; Matthew contains more exorcisms, angelic appearances, divinely inspired dreams and nature miracles than the other three Gospels.

The kingdom of heaven is the main theme of the Gospel and

Matthew uses many devices to underline its essential heavenly nature, presenting it as a kingdom which is characterised by uprightness, gentleness and meekness. Matthew shows that only the kingdom's ruler has the right to act as judge—and judgement is a secondary theme of this Gospel.

According to Matthew, there are only two ways to react to the authoritative Jesus: with obedience or rejection. If Matthew the apostle was the author, he gives his own testimony in simple words: 'As Jesus was walking on from there he saw a man named Matthew sitting at the tax office, and he said to him, "Follow me." And he got up and followed him' (9:9). This Matthew obeyed Jesus' command without question and from that and other small beginnings grew a Gospel, a Gospel of kingdom obedience.

3

Mark's View of Jesus

Mark views Jesus, not so much as a powerful king who comes to reign, but more as the suffering servant of God who comes to serve and to offer himself as a sacrifice for all humankind. Throughout his short Gospel, Mark delicately highlights small details of Jesus' life. The result is a picture of the perfect example of patient service.

Only five passages are unique to Mark's Gospel: one parable (4:26–29), two miracles (7:31–37; 8:22–26), a domestic incident (3:20–21) and some post-resurrection teaching (16:14–20). So at first glance Mark does not appear to be as distinctively different as the other three Gospels. However, a closer examination of this Gospel shows unique marks which are as conclusive and characteristic as the unmistakable differences in Matthew, Luke and John.

Though small, these marks are numerous and occur in every chapter. On its own, each can appear so faint as to be meaningless, but when the marks are grouped together, they form a series of consistent themes which gain meaning when seen from the viewpoint of service.

Jesus is

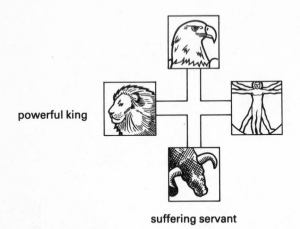

powerful king

suffering servant

MATERIAL ABSENT FROM MARK

Genealogy and nativity

Mark records no genealogy and no details about Jesus' birth and background. These are not important from the viewpoint of service, as it is not the origin of servants that matters but the work they do and how well they do it.

Mark, in contrast to the other Gospels, comes straight to service. He touches on John the Baptist but does not include the prediction added by Matthew and Luke that Jesus will burn the chaff in an unquenchable fire. He passes quickly over Jesus' baptism. He offers no details of Jesus' testing by Satan. After this very brief summary of events, Mark begins his description of Jesus' service in Galilee.

The nativity

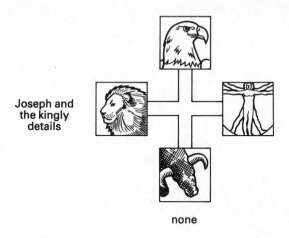

Joseph and
the kingly
details

Teaching and parables

Mark does not record any occasion when Jesus makes an
extended kingly proclamation of the laws of his kingdom, as in
the Sermon on the Mount, with the result that in this Gospel Jesus
looks more like a servant than a king.

The Lord's Prayer is not mentioned—it has no bearing on
Jesus' path of service to others. There are no long discourses, for
in Mark the service lies in doing rather than teaching. There are
only eight short parables and most of these have an obvious connection with service.

One of these parables, the story of the seed growing secretly
(4:26–29), is unique to Mark. He places this parable between the
parable of the sower (4:1–20) and the mustard seed (4:30–32),
whereas Matthew puts the parable of the darnel in the corresponding position (Mt 13:4–32). This highlights the difference
between Matthew and Mark. The parable of the darnel gives

Jesus the place of power as Lord of the harvest, but the parable of the seed growing secretly is about service, suggesting that true service should be unobtrusive and encouraging servants to work steadily in faith, leaving the results to God.

Jesus' parables illustrate

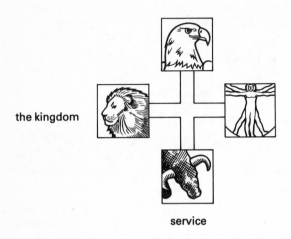

the kingdom

service

The Lord and his apostles

When Mark describes Jesus' appointment of the Twelve, he alone reports that 'they were to be his companions' (3:14). Mark always presents the apostles as Jesus' companions and he does not record them calling Jesus 'Lord' (*kurios* in Greek). In fact, the only person to address Jesus as *kurios* in Mark is a Syro-Phoenician woman and she only uses the word because she is a Gentile woman speaking to a strange Jewish man.

Where the other Gospel writers use the word *kurios*, Mark does not. For example, when the leper comes to Jesus in Matthew he says, 'Lord, if you are willing, you can cleanse me' (Mt 8:2) but in Mark he says, 'If you are willing, you can cleanse me' (1:40). In the storm, Matthew's disciples cry, 'Save us, Lord, we are lost!' (Mt 8:25), whereas Mark's disciples shout, 'Teacher, do you not care? We are lost!' (4:39). And at the Last Supper, the disciples say in Matthew's version, 'Not me, Lord, surely?' (Mt 26:22) but in Mark's, 'Not me, surely?' (14:19).

There are many different explanations for the absence of *kurios* in Mark but all agree that the consistent presence of the word in the other three Gospels, and its absence here, are not by chance. Whatever the reasons, it has the effect of magnifying Jesus' servanthood in Mark.

Judgements

In Mark's Gospel, Jesus passes few judgements on people and he does not sentence Jerusalem or Capernaum. While in Matthew Jesus indicts the scribes and Pharisees seven times (Mt 23), in Mark Jesus simply warns his followers to 'beware of the scribes' (12:38). Mark follows this warning with words (ignored by Matthew) spoken when Jesus is sitting opposite the Treasury watching a poor widow. It is as though Mark is suggesting that, if Jesus must judge, then he is looking for service and can see and appreciate the smallest gesture.

In contrast to Matthew's version of Jesus' prophecy on the Mount of Olives (Mt 24–25), Mark's account (13:3–37) includes no bridegroom receiving and rejecting the attendants, no master judging between faithful and unfaithful servants and no king separating the nations to his right and left hand. Instead, Mark (in some manuscripts), unlike Matthew and Luke, includes the Son in his list of those who do not know the day or hour of the coming of the Son of Man: just like other servants, Jesus waits to be told what he must do and when he must do it.

Passion and resurrection

At Jesus' arrest, Mark does not include a reference to Jesus' right to summon twelve legions of angels to his defence. On the cross, Mark does not record Jesus' promise of paradise made to his dying companion. And at the resurrection, Mark does not mention any miraculous earthquakes, powerful angels or resurrected saints. Again, there are different theories about why these details are omitted, but one result of their absence from Mark is that Jesus' power and authority are in the background while his suffering service is in sharper focus.

Even in the last scene, the disciples' commission, Mark differs from Matthew to draw out his distinctive emphasis. He does not record Matthew's claim that Jesus has received all authority; instead, he reports Jesus saying, 'Go out to the whole world; proclaim the gospel to all creation. Whoever believes and is baptised will be saved; whoever does not believe will be condemned' (16:15–16; this is not in all the old manuscripts of Mark). Here, Jesus is not ordering obedience to all his commands, or issuing instructions about discipling with authority, but instead he is asking for faithful service and, knowing the path of service himself, is hinting at rejection as well as success.

The ending

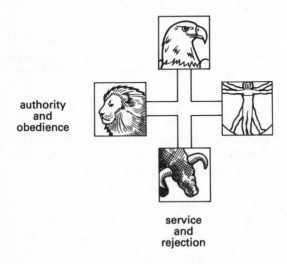

authority
and
obedience

service
and
rejection

MATERIAL EXCLUSIVE TO MARK

If, as most Protestant scholars believe, Matthew and Luke used Mark as one of their primary sources, Mark's exclusive details were either added after they had used Mark or were deliberately ignored by Matthew and Luke. Either way, this means that these details assume an extra significance as we seek to understand the Gospel writers' emphases. And nearly all of these details are facts which are only significant for a writer who is looking at everything from the viewpoint of service. It is these serving details which are systematically omitted by Matthew and Luke whenever they seem to use Mark's material.

Baptism and temptation

Significantly, Mark begins his Gospel of service by describing John as a messenger who has been sent to perform a particular task: 'Look, I am going to send my messenger in front of you to prepare your way before you' (1:2). Passing quickly over Jesus' baptism and testing, Mark mentions the fact that Jesus 'was with the wild animals' (1:13). From Matthew's kingly viewpoint, wrestling with Satan is the most important aspect of Jesus' time in the desert, whereas the most significant detail from Mark's serving viewpoint is that Jesus lives for a while with animals.

At once

Mark underlines the theme of service by frequent use of the Greek word *euthus* which is translated variously as 'at once', 'immediately', 'straightway' and 'forthwith'. *Euthus* occurs eighty times in the New Testament and forty of these are in Mark's short Gospel where the word suggests the quick response of an eager servant. Mark uses 'at once' ten times in chapter 1 to introduce the idea of immediate action. Only three of these uses are repeated in Matthew's or Luke's corresponding passages.

Key word

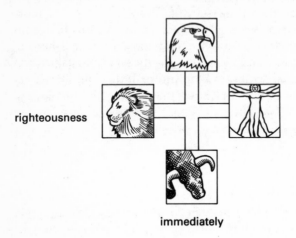

righteousness

immediately

Jesus' travels

Mark mentions several small details about Jesus' life which are omitted by Matthew and Luke in their accounts of the same incidents. They are the sort of details that are only noted by someone who has the eyes of a servant: 'he was in the house' (2:1); 'he went home again' (3:20); 'he had gone into the house' (7:17); 'when he had gone indoors' (9:28); 'he was setting out on a journey' (10:17); 'he followed him along the road' (10:52); and 'as Jesus was walking in the Temple' (11:27).

The second of these details introduces the only incident which is unique to Mark:

> He went home again, and once more such a crowd collected that they could not even have a meal. When his relations heard of this, they set out to take charge of him; they said, 'He is out of his mind' (3:20–21).

Jesus' gestures

Matthew and Luke constantly abbreviate Mark's account of particular incidents, with the result that Mark's Gospel has more detail about the way Jesus serves. Only Mark records that Jesus took Simon's mother-in-law 'by the hand and helped her up' (1:31); that he took the epileptic boy 'by the hand and helped him up' (9:27); that he 'embraced' (9:36) the little child he had set among his disciples; and 'embraced' the children his disciples had turned away (10:16). These small touches of tenderness, ignored by Matthew, highlight the theme of service.

Jesus' looks

A servant is trained to use his eyes, and Mark records the way that Jesus looked at people in passages where the other Gospels give no such information. Only Mark reports that before healing the man with the withered hand in the synagogue, Jesus 'looked angrily round at them' (3:5); that when the crowd told him his mother and brothers were outside, he was 'looking at those sitting in a circle round him' (3:34); that when he spoke of the cross and Peter began to rebuke him, Jesus 'turning and seeing his disciples . . . rebuked Peter' (8:33); that when the rich young man asked how he could inherit eternal life, Jesus 'looked steadily at him and he was filled with love for him' (10:21); and that immediately after the man had gone sadly away, Jesus 'looked round' and then spoke to his disciples (10:23).

Jesus' hiddenness

Mark describes just two miracles which are not mentioned by the other Gospel writers: the healing of a deaf man (7:31–37) and of a blind man (8:22–26). Mark uses both of these episodes to show Jesus' desire to work unobtrusively, which is surely one mark of a good servant. Jesus takes the deaf man 'aside to be by themselves, away from the crowd'. When the man can hear, Jesus instructs him 'to tell no one about it' (7:33, 36). It is the same with the blind man:

Jesus 'took the blind man by the hand and led him outside the village', and when he could see, said, 'Do not even go into the village' (8:26).

Jesus wants to serve unseen and he is ready to serve unthanked. He often asks for secrecy and the other Gospels report these requests. But they do not describe Jesus' attempts to hide himself. For example, although Matthew also mentions Jesus' visit to Tyre, only Mark notes that 'he went into a house and did not want anyone to know he was there' (7:24).

Jesus' miracles show

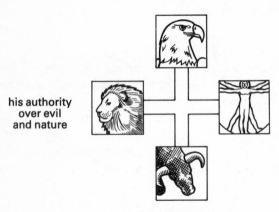

his authority
over evil
and nature

his unobtrusive service

There are many theories about the secrecy of Jesus in Mark. One popular view suggests that Jesus wanted to calm the excited Jewish crowds because they misunderstood the nature of his role as Messiah. This misunderstanding was less likely among the Gentiles, hence his call for testimony in Mark 5:19. However, it is not possible to know exactly why Jesus requested secrecy, nor is it possible to know why the secrecy is emphasised more in Mark than in the other Gospels. But one consequence of the presence of these details is that Mark gives us a view of Jesus which differs in emphasis from the other three Gospels.

Jesus and crowds

A servant is often at the beck and call of others and Mark—more than the other Gospels—shows how Jesus sometimes allows people to intrude on his privacy. Twice he notices that Jesus is so at the disposal of others that he cannot even eat (3:20; 6:31). But, more importantly, he emphasises that when crowds seek Jesus he does not turn them away. For example, Mark describes how on one occasion Jesus accedes to the crowd's demands when he is in the middle of praying.

> In the morning, long before dawn, he got up and left the house and went off to a lonely place and prayed there. Simon and his companions set out in search of him, and when they found him they said, 'Everybody is looking for you.' He answered, 'Let us go elsewhere, to the neighbouring country towns, so that I can proclaim the message there too, because that is why I came (1:35–39).

Special insights

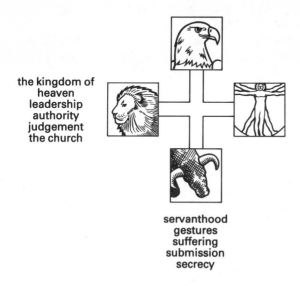

the kingdom of
heaven
leadership
authority
judgement
the church

servanthood
gestures
suffering
submission
secrecy

After the apostles' mission, Mark alone reports on Jesus' practical sympathy: 'Come away to some lonely place all by yourselves and rest for a while' (6:31). Mark goes on to describe how the crowds recognise and chase after Jesus and how the servant who has been given all the necessary resources responds: 'He took pity on them . . . and he set himself to teach them at some length' (6:34). When it gets late, the apostles want to send the crowds away hungry, but Jesus feeds them first. Then he remembers his tired apostles and 'made his disciples get into the boat . . . while he himself sent the crowd away'. But when they reached the other side, 'people at once recognised him, and started hurrying all through the countryside' (6:45, 54–55).

Jesus' motivation

Mark does not ignore Jesus' power and authority but he does refer to it more briefly than Matthew and—in one or two passages—includes some exclusive phrases which point to a secret of Jesus' power. In his first chapter, Mark describes a typical day in the life of serving Jesus: he teaches in the synagogue, ejects an evil spirit, heals Peter's mother-in-law, and relieves the sufferings of all those who come flocking round the door. Mark follows this with words which suggest one secret behind Jesus' powerful service: 'In the morning, long before dawn' (1:35) he goes off to pray.

When the leper comes to Jesus, only Mark notes that Jesus feels sorry for him (1:41). Matthew and Luke record the miracle, but it is left to Mark to reveal the compassion behind the service. Mark makes the same comment at the feeding of the five thousand (6:34) and when the rich young ruler questions Jesus, only Mark records that Jesus 'was filled with love for him' (10:21). By these and similar touches Mark suggests that true service is inspired by love and compassion.

Mark also implies that as well as love in the servant, there must be faith in the one served. For instance, only Mark explains that Jesus 'could work no miracle' in Nazareth because 'he was amazed at their lack of faith' (6:5–6). And although the story of the epileptic demoniac is also reported in Matthew and Luke, only in Mark does the boy's father cry out, 'But if you can do anything . . .' and Jesus instantly replies, 'Everything is possible for the one who has faith' (9:23–24).

Jesus' sufferings

Mark goes into more detail than the other writers about the trials suffered by Jesus. Only he reports that Jesus is 'grieved to find them so obstinate' (3:5); that Jesus has to endure his family's refusal to understand, seen in their comment, 'He is out of his mind' (3:21); that Jesus is 'amazed' at the lack of faith in his home town (6:6); that he sighs before healing (7:34); and that he talks to the Pharisees 'with a profound sigh' (8:12).

The passion emphasis

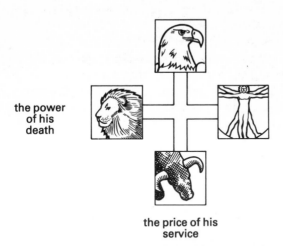

the power
of his
death

the price of his
service

Jesus' greatest suffering takes place on the cross and a deep awareness of the cross pervades Mark's Gospel. Throughout the Gospel the cross is revealed as both the price and the glory of service. In Mark, everything leads up to the moment in chapter 8 when the apostles realise who Jesus is and are ready to learn of the cross. From that point on, the theme of suffering and death is dominant in Jesus' teaching: 'The Son of Man himself came not to be served but to serve, and to give his life as a ransom for many' (10:45).

When Jesus speaks to the rich young man in Matthew and Luke, he says, 'Go and sell your possessions and give the money to the poor, and you will have treasure in heaven; then come, follow me,' but in Mark Jesus adds the extra command 'and take up the cross' (10:21, AV). Immediately after this, in answer to Peter's remonstrations, only Mark reports Jesus' promise that those who have left everything for the gospel will be rewarded with 'persecutions too' (10:30).

Mark's account of Jesus' passion does not include any details which are unreported by the other writers. Their simple story of Jesus' trial, torture, sufferings and death is entirely appropriate to Mark's view of Jesus as God's suffering servant. But Mark closes his Gospel quite differently from Matthew, Luke and John, showing in his very last sentence that Jesus is still the servant: '. . . While they, going out, preached everywhere, the Lord working with them and confirming the word . . .' (16:20, omitted by some old manuscripts). So Mark reveals that the risen Jesus, even though he is finally called 'the Lord', is still the worker. And with this characteristic small touch Mark ends the Gospel which highlights the serving face of God.

4

Luke's View of Jesus

Luke views Jesus, not primarily as a king or a servant, but more as the ideal human being, the perfect specimen of humanity, the pattern life for all humankind. This Gospel's differences show that Jesus is someone who is tested in every possible way, and is subject to ordinary conflict and emotions, yet remains without sin. Luke reveals that Jesus is a sympathetic friend of sinners and a man to be followed.

Jesus is

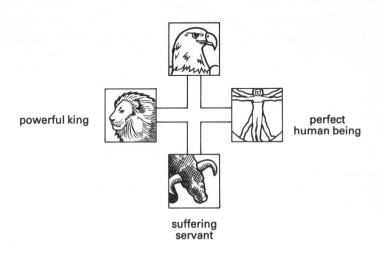

powerful king

perfect human being

suffering servant

Mark's view of Jesus has to be gathered from small details, whereas Luke's view can be seen patently on every page: his choice of material clearly underlines the perfect humanity of Jesus.

Luke begins his book by referring to his own knowledge and by addressing the Gospel to an acquaintance. It is a human beginning, and in keeping with his view of Christ.

Nativity, childhood and genealogy

Luke makes more of the events surrounding Jesus' birth than the other Gospel writers, and uses the story to introduce some of his distinctive themes: the humanity of Jesus, the place of women, the treatment of the poor, care for small children, the help of the Holy Spirit, hospitality, healing miracles, praise and joy.

In his account of the nativity (1:5–2:38), Luke shows that God wants to draw ordinary men and women to himself, to fill them with the Holy Spirit (among the Gospels, a phrase unique to Luke) and to use them in passing on good news about Jesus. In his genealogy (3:23–38), Luke traces Jesus' ancestors backwards, as most people do. He goes back to Adam, thus showing Jesus to be the brother of all humanity. And in his account of Jesus' childhood (2:39–52), Luke describes Jesus' early devotion to his heavenly Father and his subsequent submission to his earthly parents.

Only Luke reports that John the Baptist and Jesus are related. And only he features the words and actions of Zechariah, Elizabeth, Gabriel, Simeon and Anna. His nativity focuses on Mary's response to God (Joseph is almost completely ignored); on humble shepherds who visit the baby empty-handed; on the Holy Family's poverty; on three miracles which affect the elderly Zechariah; on the part played by the Holy Spirit; and on mystified Jewish teachers. Luke decorates the story with small details about everyday life which are only relevant from the human viewpoint: taxes, baby clothes, happy neighbours, two pigeons, a manger, writing materials and a frantic search for a missing child.

The nativity

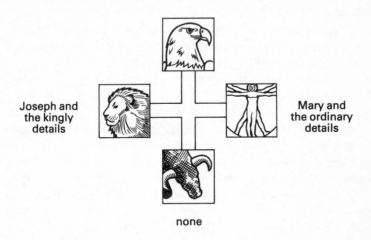

Joseph and
the kingly
details

Mary and
the ordinary
details

Joy permeates Luke's account of the nativity. The angel tells Zechariah that his son 'will be your joy and delight and many will rejoice at his birth' (1:14). The angel's first words to Mary are, 'Rejoice, you who enjoy God's favour!' (1:28). On seeing Mary, Elizabeth gives a loud cry and tells her that 'the child in my womb leapt for joy' (1:44). Mary rejoices (1:47), the neighbours share Elizabeth's joy (1:58) and Zechariah praises God (1:64). The angel brings the shepherds 'news of great joy, a joy to be shared with the whole people' (2:10). Then the hosts of heaven praise God (2:13), shepherds praise God (2:20) and elderly Anna praises God (2:38). This delightful theme of praise and joy runs right through Luke's Gospel.

Luke closes this section with an exclusive glimpse of Jesus' childhood that would be out of place in any other Gospel. Only Luke reports that Jesus 'went down with them then and came to Nazareth and lived under their authority. His mother stored up all these things in her heart. And Jesus increased in wisdom, in stature, and in favour with God and with people' (2:51–52).

Jesus the Christ

Luke makes it clear that Jesus identifies himself fully with the people of the world and their concerns. Luke alone sets the historical and political background: 'In the fifteenth year of Tiberius Caesar's reign, when Pontius Pilate was governor of Judaea . . .' (3:1–2); reports that Jesus 'was about thirty' (3:22); and describes Nazareth as the place 'where he was brought up' (4:16).

In the first part of his book Luke offers several clues to Jesus' identity and function, and presents many people who wonder who Jesus can be. The clues come from Gabriel (1:31–33), John (3:15–17), a heavenly voice (3:22) and Jesus (4:17–22). The questions are asked by the Nazareth congregation (4:23), John (7:18–20), thunderstruck disciples (8:25) and Herod (9:7–9).

Chapter 9 is the turning point in the Gospel. There Jesus asks his disciples: '"But you . . . who do you say I am?"' And Peter answers with 'the Christ of God' (9:20–21). 'Christ' is the Greek equivalent of the Hebrew word 'Messiah', and both these words mean 'anointed man'.

Jesus and money

Luke packs his Gospel with teaching about money, warnings about wealth and pleas for extreme generosity. Most chapters contain either a parable, some teaching or an incident about wealth. This is one of the Gospel's main teaching themes, and the only information Luke gives about the people he describes is whether or not they are generous. John the Baptist (3:10–11), the Capernaum centurion (7:5–6), Joanna and Susanna (8:1–3), Zacchaeus (19:8–10), the Temple widow (21:1–4) and Joseph of Arimathaea (23:50–54), all illustrate how Luke consistently commends those who give their wealth away. Nearly all of Luke's unique parables feature the use of money or possessions. Even the miracle of the bumper catch of fish is, in part, presented as an economic test: will the fishermen haul it in, then leave it on the shore for others while they themselves follow Jesus (5:1–11)?

Key word

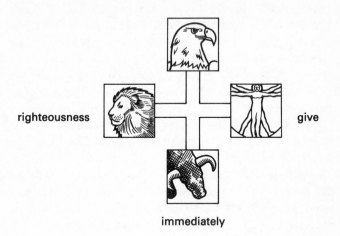

righteousness   give

immediately

Luke portrays Jesus as an ordinary, and poor, member of humanity; not someone who is independent of class, but a man who is on the side of the lowest members of society. According to Luke, Jesus' first earthly resting place is an animal feeding trough (2:16), his last is another man's grave (23:53), and in between he has nowhere to lay his head (9:58). Luke even reports that when Mary and Joseph take the baby Jesus to the Temple to present him to God, they give the special offering for the poor (2:24).

Luke's understanding of Jesus' teaching on money is perhaps best expressed in Jesus' words:

> Sell your possessions and give to those in need. Get yourselves purses that do not wear out, treasure that will not fail you, in heaven where no thief can reach it and no moth destroy it. For wherever your treasure is, that is where your heart will be too (12:33–34).

If uprightness is the most important characteristic of the kingdom from Matthew's point of view, generosity is its equivalent from Luke's.

Jesus and prayer

Luke reveals Jesus as a man of prayer. John records Jesus' longest prayer (Jn 17), and Matthew goes into more detail about the Lord's Prayer (Mt 6:5–18), but only Luke weaves prayer throughout Jesus' life and teaching.

Luke begins with a crowd of people praying outside the Temple sanctuary (1:10) and goes on to show Jesus praying at all the most important moments in his ministry: his baptism (3:21); before choosing the Twelve (6:12); when revealing himself as 'the Christ of God' (9:18); at his Transfiguration (9:28); before his arrest (22:45); and as he dies (23:46).

Luke describes Jesus visiting deserted places to pray (5:16). He mentions the occasion when Jesus spends a whole night in prayer on a mountain (6:12). He describes a disciple's request to be taught to pray (11:1). He records some unique parables and teaching about prayer (11:5–8; 18:1–14). He reports Jesus' anger at finding people profiteering in the Temple instead of praying there (19:45–46). He notes that Jesus prays for Peter's faith not to fail (22:32) and asks his disciples to pray not to be tested (22:40). And the last chapter of his Gospel has Cleopas' recognition of Jesus as he offers a prayer of blessing (24:30–31). Luke's ideal human being sets an example of prayer which his followers are meant to imitate.

Jesus and men

Luke's Gospel shows that Jesus is good news for men. By describing more ordinary men than the other three Gospels, it highlights Jesus' interest in the poor, the outcast and the commonplace. Matthew may uniquely mention the Wise Men, and John may introduce Lazarus, Nicodemus and the beggar who washes Jesus' spittle off his face, but Luke offers exclusive insights into Cleopas, Herod, Simeon, Simon, Zacchaeus, Zechariah, the shepherds, the seventy-two and the unnamed thief on the cross.

Luke emphasises that Peter, James and John are particularly

close to Jesus. These are the apostles he mentions most often; after the list in 6:12–16, Levi (Matthew) and Judas (Iscariot) are the only other members of the Twelve to whom he refers by name.

But Luke shows more clearly than the other Gospel writers that Jesus had many more than twelve followers. Luke's Gospel refers to both apostles and disciples. The disciples are a large group of men and women from whom the twelve apostles are chosen (Lk 6:13). When Luke uses the word 'disciples' he means the larger group, not just the Twelve. Luke writes more about Jesus' dealings with the mass of ordinary disciples than with the Twelve, and is the only writer to record the important fact that seventy-two disciples were sent out by Jesus to heal and preach, and that they came back 'rejoicing' (10:1–20).

Luke includes accounts of Jesus eating with two contrasting groups of people. Scribes, Pharisees and lawyers wine and dine Jesus, but only to catch him out, whereas tax-collectors and sinners host receptions for Jesus to show their friendship and support.

Luke describes five occasions when Jesus is a guest at a meal, and reveals that the ideal man, though thoroughly sociable, does not conform to expected standards of behaviour. When Levi holds a reception in Jesus' honour, the Pharisees complain and Jesus replies, 'I have come to call not the upright but sinners to repentance' (5:32). Later, a Pharisee invites Jesus to a meal, but while he is eating, Jesus becomes preoccupied with a sinner and offers her friendship and forgiveness. The other guests are outraged and accuse Jesus of profanity and arrogance (7:36–50). At the third meal, Jesus does not wash before eating, and when his host expresses surprise, Jesus launches into a series of insulting judgements upon the Pharisees (11:37–54). And at another meal with a leading Pharisee, Jesus offers some uncomfortable teaching about the Sabbath and about hospitality: 'When you have a party, invite the poor, the crippled, the lame, the blind; then you will be blessed' (14:1–14).

Throughout his Gospel, Luke introduces a series of men who respond to Jesus in contrasting ways. He places ordinary men in the centre of the nativity. He presents Gentile men in a particularly favourable light—especially centurions and soldiers. And he focuses on the involvement of ordinary people in the events surrounding Jesus' death.

Luke begins with a detailed description of God's dealings with Zechariah and ends by recounting at length Jesus' conversation with the disciple Cleopas. These two men, together with Zacchaeus, are examples of ordinary men who are changed by God. The story of Zacchaeus is typical of Luke, including as it does, repentance, generosity and hospitality, and ending on a note of great joy: 'He hurried down and welcomed him joyfully' (19:6).

Special insights

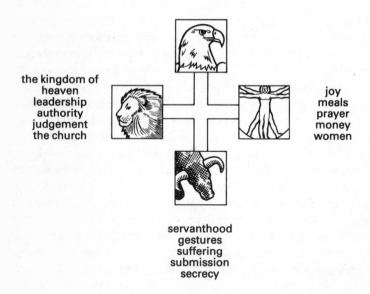

the kingdom of
heaven
leadership
authority
judgement
the church

joy
meals
prayer
money
women

servanthood
gestures
suffering
submission
secrecy

Jesus and women

Luke records nineteen incidents which feature women, whereas the other three writers only mention women in passing. Matthew and Mark refer to four stories which Luke does not include and

John also mentions four stories about women which are absent from Luke. However, Luke underlines the importance of women to Jesus by adding the following exclusive material: the parables of the lost coin (15:8–10) and the unscrupulous judge (18:1–8); the part played in the nativity by Elizabeth, Mary and Anna; the healing of the crippled woman (13:10–17); the resuscitation of the only son of the widow of Nain (7:11–17); the woman who kisses Jesus' feet (7:36–38); the women who provide for Jesus' support (8:1–3); the sisters who argue about preparing a meal for Jesus (10:38–42); and the woman who calls out in the crowd (11:27–28).

The healing of the crippled woman (13:10–17) is very characteristic of Luke. It features a woman, records precise details about her condition and her healing, mentions confrontation with the authorities, reports that the woman glorified God and ends by noting that 'all the people were overjoyed at all the wonders he worked'.

Luke always presents women warmly and favourably. He offers them as examples of perseverance and generosity, as faithful disciples and as the first witnesses to the resurrection. Jesus does not patronise women but is shown treating them as seriously as he treats men. He answers their questions, corrects their errors and applauds them when they are mocked by others. Luke does not portray any woman in conflict with Jesus, though two women are gently rebuked.

Luke shows Jesus' patience and compassion for a bereaved woman (7:11–16). He suggests that the first New Testament person to be 'filled with the Holy Spirit' is a woman (1:41). And he notes that women stay with Jesus at his death (23:49), hope to care for his body (23:55) and hear the news of the resurrection before the men (24:6). Only in Luke's human Gospel are women so prominent in the life and affections of Jesus.

Jesus' miracles

Matthew, Mark and Luke each record about twenty miracles. But Luke's selection is quite different from the other two. They record more miracles of exorcism and miracles over the forces of nature, while Luke includes more miracles of healing. Luke's emphasis on Jesus' humanity may be one reason why he is the only Gospel writer who does not mention Jesus walking on water, and this may be a reason why he does not include other similar stories which it seems probable that he knew: for example, the withered fig tree, the exorcism of the Canaanite woman's daughter and the turning of water into wine.

Luke records ten unique miracles: Elizabeth's conception (1:24); Zechariah's silence and subsequent healing (1:20–22, 64); Peter's catch of fish (5:4–7); the resuscitation in Nain (7:11–17); the miracles of the seventy-two (10:17); the cure of a crippled woman (13:10–17); the healing of the man with dropsy (14:1–6); the cure of ten lepers (17:11–19); and the restoration of a servant's severed ear (22:51).

Jesus' miracles show

his authority over evil and nature

his compassion and sympathy

his unobtrusive service

Luke claims to write an ordered account of events and, as in Mark, miracles dominate the first part of Jesus' ministry. Teaching only comes to the fore after the disciples realise that Jesus is the Christ, the anointed man. Jesus' early miracles lead to a climax of miracles in 8:22–56 and miracles are mentioned less frequently once these have been described.

All Luke's miracles focus on Jesus, but they are not all worked by Jesus. They begin with the two conceptions and end with the resurrection appearances and the ascension. Jesus' miracles lead few people to believe that he is God; instead, most people conclude that he is a tool of Satan or a prophet (anointed prophets were the only miracle-workers in the Old Testament). Luke also mentions the miracles performed by the Twelve (9:10), the itinerant exorcists (9:49–50) and the seventy-two (10:17). These stories remind Luke's readers that God can work miracles through any person he chooses, not just through Jesus; and Jesus' words to the seventy-two remind readers 'not [to] rejoice that the spirits submit to you; rejoice instead that your names are written in heaven' (10:20).

Jesus' parables

The four Gospels contain about forty different parables. John does not mention any parables, Mark refers to eight, Matthew includes twenty-one and Luke twenty-eight. Matthew's and Luke's large collections reflect their differing emphases. They have twelve parables in common, sixteen are unique to Luke and nine are found only in Matthew. Most of Matthew's exclusive parables are about 'a king', 'an owner' or a 'master', whereas Luke's are mainly about 'a certain man'. Luke's exclusive parables portray the activities of ordinary people. They are about money, possessions, debt, forgiveness, generosity, selfishness and rejoicing. They advocate humility, persistence, and prayer; refer to conflict, suffering and death; and illustrate repentance and forgiveness. And they underline the fact that God has no favourites—he cares about foreigners and all those who are ignored by Jews.

Luke's shared parables also feature the everyday activities of working people, but they illustrate different truths from his exclusive parables. They are not about his great themes of money and prayer, and they do not emphasise that God is on the side of the poor and the needy. Instead, they answer questions about the behaviour of Jesus and the responsibilities of his followers. They draw attention to the importance of obedience, the generous and forgiving nature of God's kingdom, Jesus' attitude to traditional devotional practices and his conflict with the Jewish hierarchy.

Jesus' parables illustrate

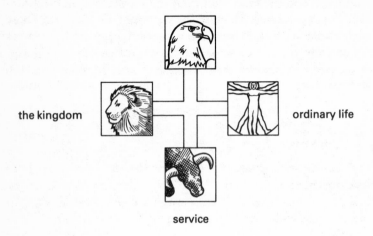

the kingdom

ordinary life

service

Five of these parables differ slightly from their parallel versions in the other Gospels. In the parable of the wineskins Luke adds the human observation that 'nobody who has been drinking old wine wants new' (5:39). Matthew uses the parable of the builders to illustrate entering God's kingdom, while Luke uses it to describe living in the kingdom (6:47). In the parable of the sower, Luke sets a higher level of spiritual reproduction (8:8), and gives a fuller description of the qualities of the good soil (8:15). Luke's shepherd goes on searching until he finds 'the lost sheep' (15:4–7), and then rejoices with his friends and neighbours—whereas Matthew's shepherd rejoices on his own and only 'if he finds it' (Mt 18:12–14). An unpopular royal claimant appears in Luke's version of the parable of the servants, and in the same parable

Luke does not send the good-for-nothing servant into outer darkness (19:11–27).

Jesus' passion and resurrection

Luke's account of the passion is essentially similar to that in the other Gospels but with a few extra exclusive details. He includes a healing miracle (22:51), Jesus' blindfold (22:64) and Jesus' wonderful conversation with the penitent thief (23:39–43). He also gives more facts about the meal, more details about Jesus' trials and more information about Peter's betrayal.

Luke's account of Jesus' ordeal does not mention Gethsemane by name. It is shorter than Matthew's and Mark's, and only describes one prayer, yet it conveys an intensity of anguish which is absent from the other accounts.

The passion emphasis

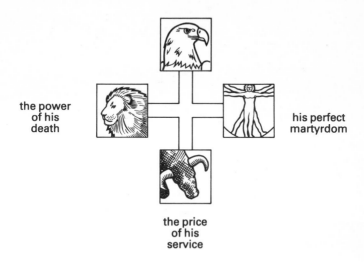

the power of his death

his perfect martyrdom

the price of his service

Luke 22:42–44 shows Jesus enduring unparalleled spiritual agony as he wrestles with his Father's will: it is Luke's most telling insight into the humanity of his perfect man.

'Father,' he said, 'if you are willing, take this cup away from me. Nevertheless, let your will be done, not mine.' Then an angel appeared to him, coming from heaven to give him strength. In his anguish he prayed even more earnestly, and his sweat fell to the ground like great drops of blood (22:42–44).

Luke's account of the crucifixion is softer than Matthew's and Mark's: his crowd is more curious than hostile, and repents at the end. Luke does not mention Jesus' desolate question about desertion; he reports that Jesus dies committing his spirit into the hands of his Father; and he shows that Jesus continues his ministry of forgiveness right to the very end. Only in Luke do we find the words, 'Father, forgive them; they do not know what they are doing' (23:34).

Throughout the passion narrative, Luke presents Jesus as an innocent man who dies as a martyr. He does not suggest any spiritual implications, applications or consequences of Jesus' death. He makes no comment about 'a ransom for many' and

The ending

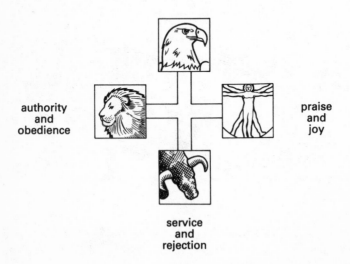

authority
and
obedience

praise
and
joy

service
and
rejection

does not mention a victory over Satan—in fact, he presents men, not Satan, as responsible for the death of Jesus. In Luke, the cross is where the anointed man fulfils his destiny by accepting and enduring rejection, suffering and death.

Luke's Gospel closes as it opens, with an angel, a miracle and disbelief by those who should know better. Luke underlines the physical reality of Jesus' risen body, and includes an appearance to an ordinary disciple. The book ends exactly where it began—in the Temple; and Luke signs off with yet more words of praise and joy.

5

John's View of Jesus

Matthew's, Mark's and Luke's three main views of Jesus result in their Gospels having a similar feel. Although their 'kingly', 'serving' and 'ordinary man' views are distinct, they are also closely related because kings, servants and ordinary men are human.

John's Gospel, however, is different. For he views Jesus not so much as the royal son of David, or as the suffering servant of God, or as the perfect example of humanity, but more as the glorious Son of God. And as God is always God, John's 'divine' Gospel has a different perspective from the three 'human' Gospels.

John's Gospel highlights the significance of what Jesus does and says. According to John, Jesus' miracles are 'signs' that can only be fully understood after Jesus' ascension; and his teaching has a deep meaning which is missed when it is first given but is appreciated later with the help of the Holy Spirit. John portrays Jesus' life in the light of this later understanding. His Gospel is a mature reflection on Jesus' words and deeds by a disciple who grasps that Jesus is fully divine, and who sees everything in this light.

Matthew wants his readers to obey the king; Mark hopes that his readers will allow his servant to serve them; Luke asks his readers to follow the perfect man; and John writes about life, light, love, truth and glory so that his readers will love and believe in God's glorious, light-bearing, life-bringing Son.

Jesus is

holy Son of God

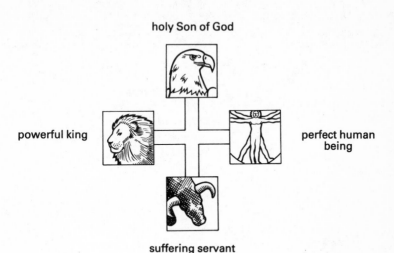

powerful king

perfect human being

suffering servant

Structure

John concentrates much more on worship than the other three writers. While Luke sets Jesus in his historical context, John relates him to the Jewish religious year. Whereas Luke records Jesus teaching at dinner parties, John presents him giving most of his sermons in the Temple. And although both Luke and John locate Jesus' miracles on journeys, John associates them with the main Jewish feasts.

To show the coming of the kingdom of heaven, Matthew structures his Gospel in seven acts around Jesus' nativity, his teaching, his miracles, his parables, the coming church, the final judgement, and Jesus' passion and resurrection.

After a short introduction, Mark constructs his Gospel around three journeys which show Jesus serving—first in Galilee; then in Tyre, Sidon, the Decapolis, Caesarea Philippi and back to Galilee; and finally, on the way through Peraea and Jericho to Jerusalem, where the passion and resurrection take place.

Luke reveals his great themes by mixing miracles, parables, teaching and narration together. Miracles introduce teaching, parables illustrate incidents, and real people are compared and contrasted with characters in parables. After describing Jesus' infancy, Luke reports on Jesus' ministry in Galilee, and then sets the bulk of his Gospel on one journey to Jerusalem.

The gospel structures

sacred feasts

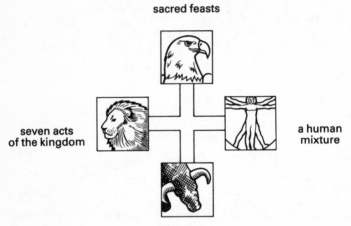

seven acts
of the kingdom

a human
mixture

three journeys

John's structure is completely different. He begins with a prologue and then builds his Gospel around the Jewish sacred feasts, dividing Jesus' life into set periods. He reports on the first week of Jesus' ministry and then on events associated with a Passover, a festival, a second Passover, a Feast of Tabernacles, a Feast of Dedication, the last week of Jesus' ministry, a third Passover and a week of resurrection appearances.

Prologue (1:1–1:18)

Matthew begins by linking Jesus with Abraham and David, and by recording the kingly version of Jesus' birth. Mark does not mention the nativity. Luke starts by telling the story of an ordinary couple and then goes on to describe Jesus' birth from Mary's human viewpoint.

John ignores Jesus' human birth and family tree, and instead, begins his Gospel with a heavenly genealogy: 'In the beginning was the Word: the Word was with God and the Word was God. He was with God in the beginning' (1:1). John uses words of astonishing beauty to describe Jesus' relationship with God, and to make it plain from the outset that Jesus is divine.

The nativity

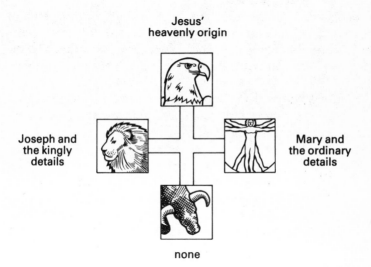

Jesus'
heavenly origin

Joseph and
the kingly
details

Mary and
the ordinary
details

John's wonderful prologue introduces themes which run right through the Gospel: 'What has come into being in him was life, life that was the light of men' (1:4); 'The Word was the real light that gives light to everyone' (1:9); 'The Word became flesh, he lived among us, and we saw his glory, the glory that he has from the Father as only Son of the Father, full of grace and truth' (1:14).

In his prologue, instead of a ruler of a kingdom, John reveals 'the light of men' (1:4); instead of a servant, he shows that 'through him all things came into being' (1:2); and instead of a man who is subject to all the problems of life, he introduces 'the only Son, who is close to the Father's heart' (1:18).

The first week (1:19–2:12)

The other three Gospels present John the Baptist's earthly relationship with Jesus, but this Gospel shows a different side of the Baptist. If Jesus is 'the light' (1:9), the Baptist is 'a lamp' (5:35) who bears witness to the light (1:8). And if Jesus is 'the Word' (1:1), the Baptist is 'a voice' (1:23) who speaks so that the Word 'might be revealed to Israel' (1:31).

In Matthew, the Baptist preaches about the kingdom of heaven. In Luke, he demands repentance evidenced by generosity. In John, he announces that 'I have seen and I testify that he is the Chosen One of God' (1:34), and proclaims, 'There is the Lamb of God' (1:35).

Matthew shows that the Baptist is reluctant to baptise Jesus because he recognises Jesus' superior authority. Luke points out that the Baptist and Jesus are relatives who must surely know each other. But John records the Baptist saying, 'I did not know him myself' (1:33). This appears to be an insurmountable discrepancy until it is grasped that John is writing about Jesus as divine Son of God, not about Jesus as man. And it is possible to know Jesus as a man and as a servant, even as a king, but not to know him as God. The Baptist knows Jesus as cousin from infancy, but he does not know him as Lamb until he sees 'the Spirit come down on him like a dove from heaven and rest on him' (1:32).

The other three Gospels move towards a climax at Caesarea Philippi when the apostles finally realise who Jesus is. But John suggests that a few of them have some understanding from the beginning: Andrew tells his brother, 'We have found the Messiah' (1:41) and Nathanael says to Jesus, 'You are the Son of God' (1:49).

John's first week ends with Jesus' first sign, the miracle at Cana. He records Jesus using words which would seem out of place in Luke: 'Woman, what do you want from me? My hour has not come yet' (2:4). (The 'hour' is the hour of Jesus' glorification on the cross and of his return to the Father's right hand.) God's glory is one of John's great themes, and throughout his Gospel he both refers to the approach of this hour (7:30; 8:20; 12:23, 27; 13:1; 17:1; 19:27) and also maintains that the miracles reveal that glory in advance—that is, they show what God is really like.

Jesus' miracles show

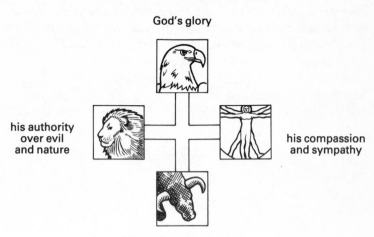

God's glory

his authority over evil and nature

his compassion and sympathy

his unobtrusive service

John also uses the miracle of the water turned into wine to hint at two ideas which he develops later in the Gospel: firstly, that human work always ends in failure but that the Son of God brings glory out of that failure; and secondly, that when human provision is exhausted, the Son of God provides an abundant supply of good things.

A first Passover (2:13–4:54)

John unveils a progression of spiritual ideas. First, he underlines the fact that the Son can restore whatever humanity ruins: 'Destroy this Temple, and in three days I will raise it up' (2:20). Second, he explains the miracle of new birth: 'No one can see the kingdom of God without being born from above' (3:3). And third, he introduces the indwelling Spirit: 'The water that I shall give him will become in him a spring of water, welling up for eternal life' (4:14).

John does not record facts because they are interesting in themselves, but to introduce a spiritual theme. He describes Nicodemus, a religious Jew, to show that, despite all his religion, Nicodemus needs new life. And he mentions a defiled Samaritan to show that, in spite of all her sin, she can contain a spring of living water. John does not record any parables, instead he includes clear teaching about his many important themes.

Jesus' parables illustrate

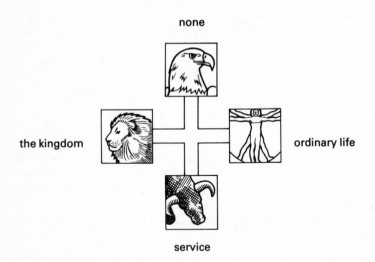

the kingdom

ordinary life

service

Many of John's themes are introduced by a unique double phrase. The other Gospels record Jesus prefacing important remarks with the Hebrew word *amen* ('verily', 'truly' or 'in truth I tell you') but only John uses a double *amen* ('verily, verily' or 'truly, truly', or 'in all truth I tell you')—and he uses this construction twenty-five times to draw attention to Jesus as Word and truth incarnate.

John makes it plain that the Son of God has come to bring life. If Matthew is concerned with righteousness and Luke with generosity, then John is preoccupied with life. And if Matthew's disciples become upright by obeying the king and Luke's disciples become generous by imitating the man, John's disciples receive eternal life by believing in the Son.

Key term

eternal life

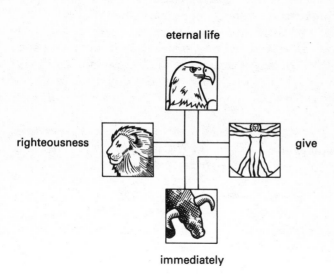

righteousness   give

immediately

John first mentions life and belief in his prologue: 'What has come into being in him was life' (1:4), and '. . . he gave power to become children of God, to those who believed in his name' (1:12). In this section, John establishes the link between life and belief with such words as 'Everyone who believes may have eternal life in him' (3:15) and, 'Anyone who believes in the Son has eternal life' (3:36). And he goes on to weave these two themes firmly together throughout the rest of his Gospel.

A festival (5:1–47)

Only John describes a healing at the Pool of Bethesda during an unspecified Jewish festival. He uses this miracle to contrast the weakness of the law with the life-giving power of the Son: just as only the strongest receive benefit from the pool, so only the strong receive help from the law. And just as the weakest are given physical strength by the Son, so anyone who believes in the Son finds eternal life: 'You pore over the scriptures, believing that in them you can find eternal life; it is these scriptures that testify to me, and yet you refuse to come to me to receive life!' (5:39).

This section contains three double *amens*, more teaching about life through belief, and the first glimmer of another of John's main themes—the equality and unity of the Father and Son: 'In all truth I tell you, by himself the Son can do nothing; he can only do what he sees the Father doing: and whatever the Father does the Son does too' (5:19).

From this point on to the end of the Gospel, John makes it clear that Jesus and the Father are one. The Son speaks what the Father says, goes where the Father sends and does what the Father is doing. By this repetition, John is not stressing Jesus' obedience to God, but is emphasising the Son's union with the Father. The Son speaks what the Father says because they are one. He does what the Father does because they exist in union. He goes where the Father sends because they cannot be separated.

A second Passover (6:1–71)

'The time of the Jewish Passover was near' (6:4). At this feast, the Jews celebrate their freedom from slavery by eating bread and roast lamb. So John sets the feeding of the five thousand in this context and records Jesus' claim, 'I am the bread of life' (6:35). This is prefaced in Greek by an emphatic *ego eimi* ('I myself, I am the bread') that recalls the name 'I am what I am' which God revealed to Moses. John uses *ego eimi* several more times in the Gospel to underline several aspects of Jesus' divinity.

There is more about life and belief in this section: '. . . whoever sees the Son and believes in him should have eternal life' (6:40); there are more double *amens*; and there is more about the oneness of the Son and the Father: 'As the living Father sent me and I draw life from the Father . . .' (6:57). But the main purpose of the section is to present Jesus as the fulfilment of the Passover. He is the living bread, he is the Lamb of God, and 'Anyone who does eat my flesh and drink my blood has eternal life' (6:54).

A Feast of Tabernacles (7:1–10:21)

John reports that on the last and greatest day of the Feast of Tabernacles, when water from the Pool of Siloam is offered to God, Jesus stands up and claims to be the fulfilment of this feast: 'Let anyone who is thirsty come to me! Let anyone who believes in me come and drink!' (7:37).

Until this feast, John has shown Jesus as life, but now he develops the theme of light. Every dusk during the feast, four golden candlesticks are lit to symbolise the pillar of fire by which God guided his people through the desert at night. And John records Jesus' claim to fulfil this aspect of the sacred feast: 'I am the light of the world; anyone who follows me will not be walking in the dark but will have the light of life' (8:12).

John uses two incidents to show the extraordinary nature of Jesus' light. An adulteress stands in the light before Jesus and is not condemned while Pharisees walk away convicted by their own consciences. And a blind man sees. Blind men are healed in the other Gospels, but only in John is the miracle introduced with the claim, 'I am the light of the world' (9:5).

John develops two ideas in this section. First, he writes about truth. Jesus says, 'If you make my word your home you will indeed be my disciples; you will come to know the truth, and the truth will set you free' (8:31–32). And second, he mentions Jesus' sacrificial death: 'I am the good shepherd: the good shepherd lays down his life for his sheep' (10:11).

A Feast of Dedication (10:22–11:57)

John follows his usual pattern of relating a sacred feast to a sign and some teaching. The eight-day Feast of Dedication celebrates the great Jewish victory under the Maccabees. It is the perfect setting for Jesus' announcement of his great victory over death which he signifies with Lazarus' resuscitation.

Here John continues to develop his themes. He writes more about belief and life: 'Anyone who believes in me, even though that person dies, will live, and whoever lives and believes in me will never die. Do you believe this?' (11:25–26). He mentions light again, '. . . anyone who walks around at night stumbles, having no light as a guide' (11:10). He stresses the theme of glory: '. . . if you believe you will see the glory of God' (11:40). He gives another *ego eimi*: 'I am the resurrection' (11:25). And he boldly underlines the essential unity of the Son and the Father: 'The Father and I are one' (10:30), and '. . . the Father is in me and I am in the Father' (10:38).

The last week (12:1–50)

In chapter 12, John describes some of the events in the last week of Jesus' life and summarises his public teaching.

John records that 'the hour has come for the Son of man to be glorified' (12:23). He restates the principle that whatever is ruined can be restored to greater glory: '. . . unless a grain of wheat falls into the earth and dies, it remains only a grain; but if it dies it yields a rich harvest' (12:24). He writes about belief, light and eternal life. He emphasises the oneness of the Son and the Father. And he presents Jesus in his divinity, as one who is served: 'If anyone serves me, the Father will honour him' (12:26). In contrast, the other three Gospels always show Jesus in his humanity, as one who has come not to be served but to serve.

The last Passover (13:1–19:42)

Most of John's Gospel is different from the other three Gospels, but John's long report of Jesus' last Passover meal is the most distinctive section of all.

John's first seven chapters are dominated by life, his next five chapters focus on light, but the rest of his book is mainly about love. John uses the word 'love' eight times in his first twelve chapters and thirty times in the last nine.

Special insights

love, light, truth and glory
unity
belief
signs and claims
new birth

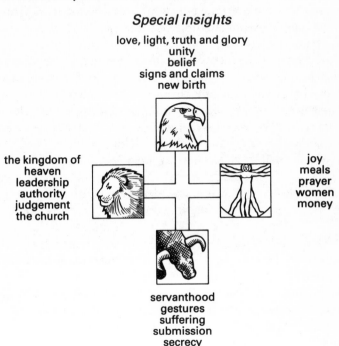

the kingdom of
heaven
leadership
authority
judgement
the church

joy
meals
prayer
women
money

servanthood
gestures
suffering
submission
secrecy

John introduces the section by showing that Jesus knows that 'his hour had come to pass from this world to the Father', and that 'having loved those who were his in the world, [he] loved them to the end' (13:1). Throughout the meal, John describes the different ways in which God expresses his love for his friends, and he shows how those friends should respond to God's love with love for God and each other.

John starts by recording the story of Jesus washing his disciples' feet. As I have already said, even though each Gospel focuses on a different face of God, the other three faces can always be seen somewhere in the background. This incident suggests the serving face of God, but John uses it primarily to illustrate the loving character of God—hence Peter's response in 13:9. John introduces the story with words which make this plain, 'Jesus knew that the Father had put everything into his hands, and that he had come from God and was returning to God, and he got up from the table, removed his outer garments and, taking a towel, wrapped it round his waist' (13:3–4).

Love dominates the Last Supper. From John's opening observations, through Jesus' teaching, right up to the very last sentence of the closing prayer, love is the theme of the meal. For example: 'I will give you a new commandment: love one another; you must love one another just as I have loved you' (13:34); '. . . whoever loves me will be loved by my Father, and I shall love him' (14:21); 'No one can have greater love than to lay down his life for his friends' (15:13); '... the Father himself loves you for loving me' (16:27); and '...so that the love with which you loved me may be in them' (17:26).

John notes more double *amens* at the meal table, more emphatic 'I am's', another reference to eternal life and, in addition to love, much about truth, glory and the oneness of the Father and the Son. Luke exclusively uses the phrase 'filled with the Holy Spirit', and he looks to earth to show the Spirit as the special help that God gives to ordinary people. But John records Jesus' clearest teaching about the Holy Spirit, and he looks to heaven to reveal the Spirit as 'the Spirit of truth who issues from the Father' (15:26). John identifies the Spirit as 'the Spirit of truth' (14:17), and introduces his work as teacher, reminder and witness.

One difference between John and the other three Gospels is Jesus' attitude towards his passion. John records Jesus standing above his sorrows, whereas the other writers focus on Jesus' human anguish and sorrow. For example, Luke's Gospel shows Jesus telling the Twelve that he 'will be handed over to the gentiles and will be mocked, maltreated and spat on' (Lk 18:32). Whereas in John's Gospel, instead of sharing his griefs with the apostles, Jesus comforts them, and says, 'Peace I bequeath to you, my own peace I give you, a peace which the world cannot give, this is my gift to you' (14:27).

The passion emphasis

his peaceful divine majesty

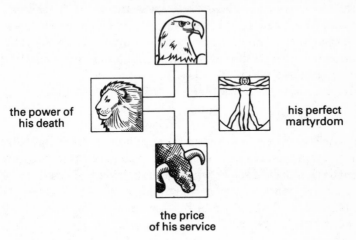

the power of
his death

his perfect
martyrdom

the price
of his service

It is the same in the garden. While Luke describes an anguished Jesus preparing for the cross, John makes no mention of the struggle with the Father's will, the strengthening angel, the bloody sweat and the human need for company and sympathy. Instead, he presents a peaceful Jesus who is fully in control of the situation: 'Knowing everything that was to happen to him, Jesus came forward and said, "Who are you looking for?" They answered, "Jesus the Nazarene." He said, "I am he" [the divine name] . . . they moved back and fell on the ground' (18:4–6). In John, instead of weakness and agony, there is peace, power, mystery and majesty.

Only John records Jesus' discussion with Pilate about truth. John makes little of the mockery and scourging, but notes the Jews' verdict that 'he ought to be put to death, because he has claimed to be the Son of God' (19:7).

John's distinctive emphasis is even seen when Jesus is dying on the cross. John does not include Jesus' words, 'My God, my God, why have you forsaken me?' (Mt 27:46) or, 'Father, into your hands I commit my spirit' (Lk 23:46). Instead, John describes Jesus' composure and assurance: 'Jesus knew that everything had been completed and, so that the scripture should be completely fulfilled, he said, "I am thirsty" . . . After Jesus had taken the wine he said, "It is fulfilled"; and bowing his head he gave up his spirit' (19:28–30). He ends his description of the passion by stating, 'This is the evidence of one who saw it . . . and he gives it so that you may believe as well' (19:35–36).

The week of resurrection (20:1–21:25)

John selects different resurrection appearances from the other three writers. He seems to give his personal testimony to the resurrection as the disciple 'whom Jesus loved' (20:2). He records Jesus' three words of peace, his sending of the disciples 'As the Father sent me' (20:21) and his breathing of the Holy Spirit (20:22).

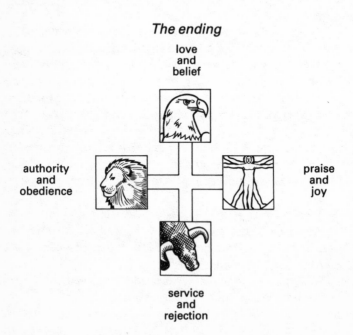

The ending

love
and
belief

authority
and
obedience

praise
and
joy

service
and
rejection

Then John brings his Gospel to a climax of belief, life and love. He records Jesus urging Thomas not to be 'unbelieving any more but believe' to which Thomas replies with words of belief which John surely hopes all his readers will share: 'My Lord and my God!' (20:27–28). And John concludes with his reason for writing the Gospel: 'These are recorded so that you may believe that Jesus is the Christ, the Son of God, and that believing this you may have life in his name' (20:30–31).

However, it is as though, having written the conclusion, somebody feels compelled to add a postscript about love. So the Gospel offers another reminder that human work always ends in failure, another example of the Son bringing glory out of failure, another miracle in which the Son lavishly provides for people whose supply is exhausted, and it ends with three last questions about love.

Matthew closes with the king's declaration of absolute authority; Mark finishes by showing that the servant is still working with his disciples; Luke ends with the perfect man's promise to send more help to his followers—and John concludes by showing that the divine Son of God is still looking for love.

6

Conclusion

As we have seen, each Gospel does differ from the other three Gospels. Each has its own viewpoint which can be seen most clearly in the material that is unique to that Gospel. Each one contains special words, themes and insights. And each one begins and ends in ways that reflect its distinctive emphases.

But there is only one Jesus, only one God, only one cross and only one gospel. The differences between the four Gospels do not leave us with four different Christs, but reveal one Jesus in four different ways. And we think it is vital that Jesus is known, worshipped and proclaimed in all of these four ways, without overemphasising one aspect or ignoring another.

Readers who grasp that the four Gospels do more than supplement and corroborate each other will find that a goldmine of study opens in front of them. Once they can see why a passage is included in one Gospel and not in another, they will discover that it assumes a much deeper meaning than they had ever realised. They will start to appreciate the significance of the variations in an event or sermon which is reported by more than one Gospel. On hearing a passage read they will begin to recognise which Gospel it comes from. And when listening to a talk they will know which Gospel viewpoint is being urged—and what complementary viewpoints need to be added so that an unbalanced response is avoided.

A summary of the emphases seen in the differences between the four Gospels

	Jesus is:	the nativity:	key words:	special insights:	Jesus' parables illustrate:	Jesus' miracles show:	the passion emphases:	the endings:
Matthew	powerful king	Joseph and the kingly details	righteous-ness	kingdom of heaven authority leadership judgement the church	the kingdom	authority over evil and nature	the power of his death	authority and obedience
Mark	suffering servant	none: it is not important for a servant	immediately	servanthood gestures suffering submission secrecy	service	his unobtrusive service	the price of his service	service and rejection
Luke	perfect human being	Mary and the ordinary details	give	joy meals prayer women money	ordinary life	his compassion and sympathy	his perfect martyrdom	praise and joy
John	holy Son of God	Jesus' heavenly origin as the eternal Word	eternal life	love, light, truth & glory unity belief signs/claims new birth	none: Jesus makes clear claims instead	God's glory	his peaceful divine majesty	love and belief

EXERCISES FOR PART ONE

The following exercises will help you to begin this sort of study and to check how well you have grasped the general principles set out in Part One.

1. Bearing in mind the differences between the Gospels, allocate the following passages to their correct Gospels. Each passage occurs in only one Gospel.

Please tick one			
Mt	Mk	Lk	Jn

a 'With him went the Twelve, as well as certain women who had been cured of evil spirits and ailments: Mary surnamed the Magdalene, from whom seven demons had gone out, Joanna the wife of Herod's steward Chuza, Susanna, and many others who provided for them out of their own resources.'

b 'If I am not doing my Father's work, there is no need to believe me; but if I am doing it, then even if you refuse to believe in me, at least believe in the work I do; then you will know for certain that the Father is in me and I am in the Father.'

c 'And at once on leaving the synagogue, he went with James and John straight to the house of Simon and Andrew. Now Simon's mother-in-law was in bed and feverish, and at once they told him about her.'

d 'Just at this time, filled with joy by the Holy Spirit, he said, "I bless you, Father, Lord of heaven and of earth, for hiding these things from the learned and the clever and revealing them to little children."'

e 'Then they brought to him a blind and dumb demoniac; and he cured him, so that the dumb man could speak and see. All the people were astounded and said, "Can this be the son of David?"'

f 'So I tell you this, that for every unfounded word people utter they will answer on Judgement Day, since it is by your words you will be justified, and by your words condemned.'

	Mt	Mk	Lk	Jn

g 'Jesus said, "This sickness will not end in death, but it is for God's glory so that through it the Son of God may be glorified."'

h 'He took the blind man by the hand and led him outside the village. Then, putting spittle on his eyes and laying his hands on him, he asked, "Can you see anything?"'

i 'In all truth I tell you, unless a grain of wheat falls into the earth and dies, it remains only a single grain; but if it dies it yields a rich harvest.'

j 'How is it that the scriptures say about the Son of man that he must suffer grievously and be treated with contempt?'

k 'For I tell you, if your uprightness does not surpass that of the scribes and Pharisees, you will never get into the kingdom of Heaven.'

l 'So in the same way, none of you can be my disciple without giving up all that he owns.'

(Check your answers with Mt 5:20; 12:22–23; 12:36–37; Mk 1:29–30; 8:23; 9:12b; Lk 8:1b–3; 10:21; 14:33; Jn 10:37–38; 11:4; and 12:24.)

2 The feeding of the five thousand is the only one of Jesus' miracles to be recorded in all four Gospels. The four accounts are substantially the same, but there are some typical differences. Bearing in mind the general principles explained in Part One, allocate the following unique facts to the appropriate Gospels:

a Jesus knew in advance exactly what he was going to do.

b The crowd was larger than 5,000.

c Jesus told the disciples to get all the people to sit on the green grass in squares of hundreds and fifties.

d Jesus personally handed the food to the crowds.

(Check your answers with Mt 14:15–21; Mk 6:35–44; Lk 9:12–17; and Jn 6:5–13.)

3 The parable of the Sower is recorded in Matthew, Mark and Luke. Again the accounts are almost exactly

	Mt	Mk	Lk	Jn

the same, but allocate these small unique details to the correct Gospels.

a The rich soil is people with a noble and generous heart.

b The seed is the word of the kingdom.

c The good soil produced a hundredfold crop. (The other two Gospels suggest it produced thirty, sixty or a hundred-fold.)

d The seed is the word.

e The people who are the rich soil yield a harvest through their perseverance.

f The seed is the word of God.

(Check your answers with Mt 13:3–23; Mk 4:3–20; and Lk 8:5–15.)

4 The mission of the Twelve is mentioned in Matthew, Mark and Luke. Which Gospels record these words of Jesus?

a 'Take nothing for the journey.'

b 'Cure the sick, raise the dead, cleanse those suffering from virulent skin-diseases, drive out devils.'

Which Gospels state that the Twelve:

c '. . . were to be his companions and to be sent out to proclaim the message.'

d were told 'as you go, proclaim that the kingdom of Heaven is close at hand'.

e were sent out 'to proclaim the kingdom of God and to heal'.

And which Gospels report that:

f 'the apostles gave him an account of all they had done'.

g 'on the Day of Judgement it will be more bearable for Sodom and Gomorrah' than for a town which rejects the Twelve.

(Check your answers with Mt 10:1–16; Mk 3:13–19; and Lk 9:1–10.)

	Mt	Mk	Lk	Jn

5 Only one Gospel describes Jesus as a carpenter; which is it most likely to be?

(Compare Mt 13:55; Mk 6:3; and Lk 4:22–23.)

6 The stilling of the storm is reported by Matthew, Mark and Luke.

a In two accounts the disciples call Jesus 'Master'; which is the account where they call him 'Lord'?

b Two accounts describe a violent storm followed by a great calm; which Gospel reports on a squall followed by calm?

c Which account reports that Jesus lay in the stern with his head on a cushion, and that they were with other boats?

(Check your answers with Mt 8:23–27; Mk 4:35–41; and Lk 8:22–25.)

7 The parable of the wicked tenants appears in Matthew, Mark and Luke.

a In two of the accounts Jesus' hearers say that the tenants deserve a harsh judgement. In which account do they say 'God forbid' at the suggestion of judgement?

b Two accounts describe a story about a man. Which account describes a landowner?

(Check with Mt 21:33–41; Mk 12:1–9; and Lk 20:9–16.)

8 The incident of Jesus walking on water is reported by Matthew, Mark and John.

a Which Gospel notes that Jesus saw the disciples were hard pressed in rowing?

b Which Gospel reports Peter's adventure, and the disciples bowing down before Jesus?

(Check with Mt 14:22–33; Mk 6:47–51; and Jn 6:19–21.)

9 The following passages follow Jesus' temptation in Matthew, Mark and Luke. Which passage belongs to which Gospel?

	Mt	Mk	Lk	Jn

a 'Jesus went into Galilee. There he proclaimed the gospel from God saying, "The time is fulfilled, and the kingdom of God is close at hand. Repent, and believe the gospel."'

b 'Jesus, with the power of the Spirit in him, returned to Galilee; and his reputation spread throughout the countryside. He taught in their synagogues and everyone glorified him.'

c 'From then onwards Jesus began his proclamation with the message, "Repent, for the kingdom of Heaven is close at hand."'

(Check with Mt 4:17; Mk 1:14–15; and Lk 4:14–15.)

10 The healing of Simon Peter's mother-in-law is reported by Matthew, Mark and Luke.

a In which Gospel is Jesus seen to take her by the hand and help her up?

b Two Gospels describe her serving 'them'. Which account reports that she served 'him'?

c After the healing which Gospel suggests that Jesus cured all the sick?

d Which one states that he healed many sick?

e Which one reports that he cured each one individually?

(Check your answer with Mt 8:14–16; Mk 1:29–34; and Lk 4:38–40.)

Practical application

The insights gained from this sort of study will not be stale theories which end only in pride. Rather, they will be shining lights which scatter darkness, and vibrant sources of life which strengthen faith and bring about a love-inspired transformation of worship, prayer, evangelism and Christian relationships.

For only when we understand that each Gospel needs the other three for the full truth about Jesus to be communicated accurately, will we be convinced that our own view of Jesus must be complemented by the views of believers who come from quite different Christian traditions.

PART TWO

7

Old Testament Foreshadowings

When second-century church leaders collected together the component parts of the New Testament, they concluded that the four Gospels, called Matthew, Mark, Luke and John, were the only authoritative accounts of Jesus' life. At that time they believed that the number four suggested fullness and completion, so it was significant to them that they could find four authoritative accounts.

During the third century, the fourfold character of the gospel became one of the accepted facts of Christianity. That Jesus should be revealed in four ways was as self-evident then as the fact that there must be four quarters of the world, four winds of heaven and the four elements of earth, wind, fire and water. By the end of that century theologians had discovered that the Old Testament contained many foreshadowings of Jesus' fourfold nature, and these were proof to them that the Holy Spirit had inspired four distinctive accounts of Jesus' life and death. From that time on, most church leaders understood and interpreted the four Gospels in terms of Old Testament imagery.

Each of the main faces of God—powerful king, suffering servant, perfect human being, holy God—can be seen on their own in many different parts of the Old Testament, either in descriptions of God, or in prophecies about the Messiah, or in people whose lives point to God. The fourfold principle can also be seen in several places where it is not possible to align the four parts with the main faces of God: for example, the four promises of

God in Exodus 6:6–7 which were represented by the four cups of the Passover. So readers must remember that the fourfold principle is always a general principle and never a fixed rule. However, there are many obvious examples of the fourfold principle in the Old Testament where four parts do relate to the four main aspects of God's nature, and this chapter examines some of these.

The first Old Testament foreshadowing of Jesus' fourfold nature is found in Eden, and it launches the idea that when God reveals something important about himself he does it in four different ways. 'A river flowed from Eden to water the garden, and from there it divided to make four streams' (Gen 2:10). There was only one river in Eden, but outside Eden it flowed in four directions to bring life and fertility to the earth.

Four names

One of the most important ways in which God reveals himself in the Old Testament is by his name. A name in the Scriptures is more than a convenient label, for it describes the nature of a person; and as God's nature is extraordinarily rich, over three hundred names are used to describe him.

There are three Hebrew words for God: *Elohim*, *Adonai*, and *Yahweh*. (*Elohim* is always translated as 'God', and is always written in English translations in lower case letters. *Adonai* is always translated as 'Lord', and is also always written in lower case. *Yahweh* is the most common word for God, and it is always written in capital letters, and is translated as either 'LORD' or 'GOD'.) These three root-words are combined with over three hundred different names to reveal the totality of God's nature, but nearly all of these names are used only once or twice in the course of the Old Testament. However, four names appear with much greater frequency than all the others: *Yahweh Sabaoth*, *El Elyon*, *El Shaddai*, and *El Qodesh*. It is the fourfold principle in action; there is only one God in heaven, but he reveals his nature on earth in four different ways. As will be shown, these four main aspects of God are also revealed in the Old Testament in priestly costume, Tabernacle furnishings, bloody offerings, public offices and prophetic visions.

The four names

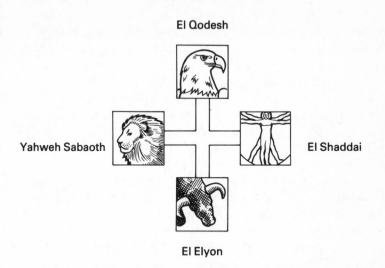

El Qodesh

Yahweh Sabaoth

El Shaddai

El Elyon

N.B. From now on, the sides of the diagrams no longer necessarily correspond with any one Gospel. Instead they correspond with the four main faces, aspects or viewpoints of God.

Yahweh Sabaoth (or *Sabaoth*) is usually translated as 'the LORD of Hosts', and it suggests that God is the leader of a large and powerful heavenly army. It is a military title which is normally used in the Old Testament to present God as all-powerful. It portrays the side of God's nature which fights battles, defeats enemies and establishes a kingdom.

This name is used most often by King David (for example, 1 Sam 17:45) and appears most frequently in the books of Samuel, Kings, Chronicles, Psalms and in the works of prophets, like early Isaiah, who were active when Israel and Judah were ruled by kings. It reveals the kingly face of God.

El Elyon (or *Elyon*) is generally translated as 'the Most High'. It suggests that God serves his people by preserving them from all kinds of harm. It is the Old Testament title which presents God as all-protecting, and was first used in connection with

Melchizedek, who was 'a priest of God Most High' (Gen 14:18).

Not surprisingly, this is Daniel's favourite name for God; and it occurs most commonly in the second and third Books of Psalms. Although *El Elyon* is the least common of the four main names, so many of the three hundred and more lesser names are linked to it, that in the Old Testament protection is the concept most commonly associated with God's name and God's nature.

El Shaddai (or *Shaddai*) is usually translated as 'the Almighty'. However, it is difficult to justify this translation linguistically, and impossible to justify it from the way it is used in its Old Testament contexts. Scholars agree that nobody can be certain exactly what *Shaddai* means and most believe that 'Almighty' is an inaccurate and inappropriate translation. (The New International Version translates both *Sabaoth* and *Shaddai* as 'Almighty', and only distinguishes between them in the footnotes.)

The Hebrew word for breasts is *shad*, so one possible translation of *Shaddai* is 'breasted'. And as *El* is a shortened version of *Elohim*, *El Shaddai* could mean the 'breasted God'. This translation makes sense when it is seen that *El Shaddai* is almost always used in the Old Testament in the context of God's provision. This name reveals God as all-providing, it introduces the mother love of God, and it points to God's feminine side. It suggests that God is like a mother who prefers to breast-feed her children, and it presents a God who lavishly provides for all his family.

El Shaddai is the name which God used when he introduced himself to Abraham and promised to provide him with an enormous family: 'I am El Shaddai. Live in my presence, and I shall grant a covenant between myself and you, and make you very numerous . . . You will become the father of many nations' (Gen 17:1–5). This name is mainly used in Genesis, Ruth and Job, always in the context of provision, and it shows God's interest in the concerns of ordinary people, especially courtship, infertility, pregnancy and birth—interests which reveal God's human face.

El Qodesh (or *Qodesh*) is normally translated as 'the Holy One'. God revealed this holy side of his nature in Leviticus 11:44–45; and the oft-repeated name 'the Holy One' or 'the Holy One of Israel' states that God is distinct from his creation—set apart by his moral perfection. It suggests that he may not be approached by those who are morally flawed. It is a spiritual title which appears most often in Leviticus, Psalms, Isaiah and Ezekiel and clearly shows the holy face of God.

Four colours

The four faces of God are so important that God ordained a dramatic and colourful visual aid which had the effect of pointing to his fourfold nature. Exodus 25:1–40:38 records the detailed instructions which God gave to Moses for the construction of the holy Tabernacle and the priestly garments. These all had to be made from fine linen, dull white in colour, which was decorated with blue, purple and scarlet yarn.

The Tabernacle colour scheme

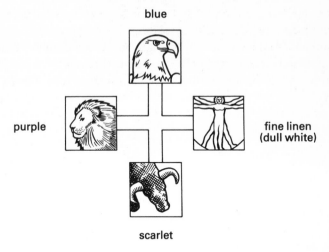

blue

purple

fine linen
(dull white)

scarlet

These four colours dominated the Tabernacle itself (Ex 26:1; 36:8), the curtain which divided the Holy Place from the Holy of Holies (26:31; 36:35), the screen at the entrance to the Tabernacle (26:36; 36:37), the screen at the entrance to the court which surrounded the Tabernacle (27:16; 38:18), the high priest's sacred vestments (28:5; 39:1), the ephod (28:6; 39:2), the breastplate of judgement (28:15; 39:8), the high priest's robe (39:22–24) and the ordinary priests' robes (39:27–29).

Only a blind Jew could worship God without noticing the colour scheme which declared 'four' as boldly and beautifully as possible. But the colours did not only suggest 'four', they also prophetically pointed to the four sides of God's nature: they were not chosen by a Mosaic whim, but by a spiritual revelation which underlined the nature of God.

Throughout the centuries, purple has always been the traditional colour of powerful kings and of their authority. Scarlet is the colour of blood, of sacrifice, of life laid down in service. Fine linen is the very best version of the material worn by ordinary men and women. And blue is the colour of the unclouded heavens where the holy God was thought to live.

These four colours filled the most sacred of all Jewish places: the place of sacrifice, priests, worship and prayer, the place where God revealed his glory to his high priest. They hinted at God's fourfold nature, and suggested that worship, sacrifice and prayer should reflect this. But most important of all, the colours pointed to the four great aspects of Jesus—powerful king, suffering servant, finest ordinary human and glorious heavenly Son of God.

Four bloody offerings

Speaking from the four-coloured Tabernacle, God gave Moses clear instructions about the offering of sacrifices, and laid down that four offerings had to be made which involved the shedding of blood: the wholly-burnt offering (Lev 1; 6:8–13), the peace offering (Lev 3; 7:11–21), the sin offering (Lev 4:1–5:13; 6:24–30) and the reparation offering (5:14–26; 7:1–10).

These sacrifices were offered personally and nationally, privately and publicly, regularly and as special needs arose. There were weekly, monthly and annual public sacrifices in the Tabernacle (and later in the Temple); and the Passover was celebrated privately within the family home. Sacrifices were offered to fulfil a vow, and to release a man from a vow; as a spontaneous act of worship; at the purification of a woman after childbirth, and of a leper; at the ordination of a priest, and at the offering of a Levite to God; at times of national repentance, and at impending battle; at royal coronations; at the dedication of sanctuaries. Whatever the reason, whenever the people turned to God, they worshipped him by offering sacrifices. The four types of bloody offerings were another pointer to the fourfold nature of God.

The bloody offerings

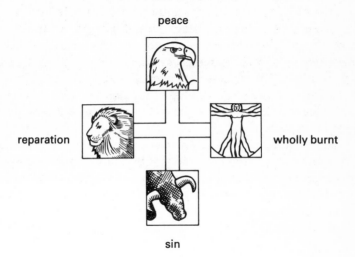

vow, and to release a man from a vow; as a spontaneous act of

Each of the four bloody sacrifices had a special use and purpose. The wholly-burnt offering and the peace offering were used in celebration and thanksgiving, in the consecration of persons and things for holy service and in the removal of ceremonial uncleanness. The sin and reparation offerings were used to effect atonement and to make restitution—that is, to cover up the worshippers' sin and to make amends for their lawbreaking.

The wholly-burnt offering represented the dedication by a person, and the acceptance by God, of everything that the worshipper had and was. The whole of this offering ascended as an aroma pleasing to God—it was all for him. This suggests the Gospel of Luke's emphasis on generosity, and the view of Jesus as a human being who lives a perfect life and burns himself out in consecration to God's will.

The eating together by priest and people of the peace offering reminded them of the vital relationship between creature and Creator, and emphasised the importance of living in close communion with God. It hints at the Gospel of John's stress on Jesus as the Son who lives his life in complete union with the Father.

Both the sin and the reparation offerings enabled the people to display their human sense of separation from a holy God, a separation caused by their sin and guilt, and to cry to him for it to be covered. But the reparation offering was more concerned with making restitution for wrongs, and the sin offering with atoning for breaking God's commandments. The reparation offering suggests Matthew's stress on upright living and the sin offering foreshadows Mark's emphasis on Jesus' death as a ransom for many.

None of these offerings, however correctly or sincerely offered, could ever permanently take away sin or fully achieve its object. They were merely a temporary institution which awaited the one whose offering on a cross would eternally fulfil each of the four bloody offerings.

Four offices

The Old Testament can be thought of as a kind of canvas on which the Holy Spirit developed the four great ways he wants people to look at God and at Jesus. It deals particularly with prophets, priests, rulers (judges, then kings) and ordinary people. These four groups of people prepared Israel for the kind of Messiah they should expect, and provide Christians with a more detailed understanding of the Christ than the New Testament alone can give.

The prophets were chosen by God; they were called into his presence; empowered by his Spirit; and inspired by his word to pass on God's truth to men and women. There were true and false prophets; obedient and disobedient prophets; great prophets who revealed much about God and lesser prophets who passed on very little information. The Old Testament prophets prepared the way for the holy Son, for the Prophet who was in the Father's presence from before the beginning, who was the Word and truth incarnate, and who fully and perfectly revealed God for all time, without any of the limitations or failings of the Old Testament prophets.

The four main offices

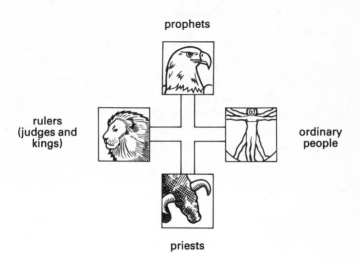

prophets

rulers (judges and kings)

ordinary people

priests

The priests were descended from Aaron; they were called to serve God in the Temple; and their lives were centred around the bloody ritual sacrifices. Hebrews 3–10 draws out the limitations of the Aaronic priesthood, and contrasts it with the incomparable greatness of Jesus as the great High Priest in the order of Melchizedek. His service, unlike that of Aaron's priests, is for ever; he does not just cover sin, he totally removes it; and he does not die out like the Old Testament priests, but lives on for ever to guarantee eternal acceptance by God. The Old Testament priesthood, even with all its imperfections, foreshadows this serving side of

Jesus, and enables believers more fully to understand and appreciate his priestly work which protects them from God's wrath.

The rulers were, at first, judges who were chosen by God and empowered by his Spirit; later, they were kings who were descended from David. There were good rulers like some of the kings of Judah, and evil rulers like all the kings of Israel after the division of the kingdom. Some ruled for a great many years, others only for a few days. Some had a great variety of gifts, others were incompetent. Some petty kings ruled only a tiny kingdom, whereas the Persian Ahasuerus governed 127 provinces. All together, the Old Testament rulers prepared the way for the rightful, wise, loving, eternal and all-powerful ruler of the whole universe.

And ordinary people appear on almost every page of the Old Testament—some with many vices, others with obvious virtues, but all of them flawed in some way. They foreshadow the one perfect man, whose unblemished life and character stands out in contrast to all other people and provides an example for all humanity to follow.

The builders of the Temple

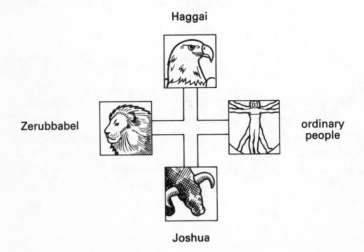

Haggai

Zerubbabel

ordinary people

Joshua

Some parts of the Old Testament focus on one particular office, for example, on kings in Kings, on prophets in Isaiah, on ordinary people in Job and on priests in Leviticus. However, other parts show that the four are vital to each other, for example, in Haggai, where the rebuilding of the Jerusalem Temple after the long years of exile is described. The first chapter of Haggai makes it plain that all four kinds of people were needed for the successful accomplishment of this important work.

There was Haggai the prophet, whose task was to live close enough to God to hear his word, and then to go and challenge those in authority to take action. Then there was Zerubbabel the governor, whose role was to give authority for the work to proceed and provide some of the materials. The project could not have succeeded without the blessing of Joshua the high priest. And it would have been impossible without a great host of ordinary people who set to and got the job done. It is an example of the fourfold principle, and foreshadows Jesus, the living temple of God who was destroyed by man and rebuilt by God. He fulfilled every one of these four offices; and he built his church, the new temple of God, on a similar fourfold pattern.

Four views of the Messiah

The Old Testament contains many different prophecies about the promised Messiah. Four of them are introduced in the Authorised Version by the word 'Behold!', and these suggest the four main views of the Messiah. Modern versions change 'behold' to either 'look', 'see' or 'here is' (though 'look carefully at' is perhaps more accurate). But 'behold' remains a more compelling word in English, so in the following quotations it replaces its counterpart in the New Jerusalem Bible.

Zechariah tells the people to rejoice and to look carefully at the approaching king: 'Rejoice heart and soul, daughter of Zion! Shout for joy, daughter of Jerusalem! *Behold*, your king is approaching, he is vindicated and victorious, humble and riding on a donkey, on a colt, the foal of a donkey' (Zech 9:9). Zechariah asks the people to meditate on the king; he focuses on his triumph and victory, shows that he is characterised by humility and gentleness, and goes on to make clear that his kingdom 'will proclaim peace to the nations, his empire will stretch from sea to sea, from the River to the limits of the earth' (9:10). This foreshadows the kingly view of Jesus. Only Matthew records this prophecy and shows that Jesus literally fulfilled it by riding into Jerusalem on a donkey and a colt.

Israel's Messiah

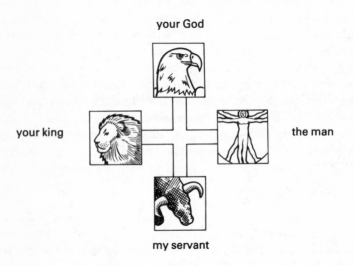

Through Isaiah, God tells the Jews to take a careful look at his servant: '*Behold* my servant whom I uphold' (42:1). He is a servant who 'does not cry out or raise his voice, his voice is not heard in the street; he does not break the crushed reed or snuff the faltering wick' (42:2). This introduces the first of the four songs in Isaiah 42–53 which describe the appalling sufferings of God's servant and are the clearest Old Testament prophetic description of Jesus' death on the cross. They foreshadow the view of Jesus as a suffering servant who gives his life as a ransom for many.

Zechariah also encourages the people to look carefully at the human face of God when he writes: 'Yahweh Sabaoth says this: '*Behold* the man whose name is Branch; where he is, there will be a branching out (and he will rebuild Yahweh's sanctuary)' (Zech 6:12). Interestingly, Zechariah goes on to show that this man will be clothed with royal majesty, and will be a priest—thus foreshadowing the close association of the different emphases in Matthew, Mark and Luke.

Finally, Isaiah instructs the messenger to tell the towns of Judah to take a careful look at their God: 'Shout as loud as you can, messenger of Jerusalem! Shout fearlessly, say to the towns of Judah, "*Behold* your God"' (Is 40:9). According to Isaiah, he is a God who 'is like a shepherd feeding his flock, gathering lambs in his arms, holding them against his breast and leading to their rest the mother ewes' (Is 40:11). Isaiah goes on to describe God's majesty and to ask, '"To whom can you compare me, or who is my equal?" says the Holy One [*Qodesh*]' (40:25). This clearly foreshadows the divine view of Jesus as holy God. Not surprisingly, it is John's Gospel which describes Jesus as the Good Shepherd who knows his sheep and keeps them safe, who feeds his followers with food which ends hunger and brings eternal life, and who wants his followers to be involved in the tasks of feeding his lambs and looking after his sheep.

Isaiah's Messiah

Isaiah 9:6 is one of the clearest of the Old Testament prophecies about the coming of the Messiah and what he will be for his people. Once again the revelation of his name and nature is fourfold:

> For a son has been born for us, a son has been given to us, and dominion has been laid on his shoulders; and this is the name he has been given, 'Wonder-Counsellor, Mighty-God, Eternal-Father, Prince-of-Peace'.

First, the Messiah will be the people's Wonder-Counsellor. Some translators use the word 'wonderful' with its overtones of beauty, but the Hebrew word *pele* means 'miracle' and is used in the Old Testament to describe the miracles or wonders of God. The use of *pele* here means that the Messiah will be a miraculous or wonder-working counsellor. In the New Testament the Holy Spirit is called the *parakletos,* a Greek word which is often translated 'counsellor' and literally means the one who is 'called alongside'—hence its other translations as 'advocate', 'companion', 'encourager' and 'comforter'. This part of the Messiah's name seems to foreshadow the Christ as the human being who can be confidently called on at any time, the never-failing, deeply sympathising friend.

Isaiah's Messiah

Mighty-God

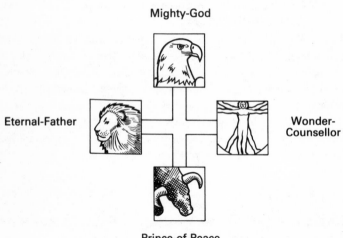

Eternal-Father

Wonder-Counsellor

Prince-of-Peace

Isaiah also says that the Messiah will be the people's Mighty-God. This was an astonishing prediction in a monotheistic society where *Yahweh* was clearly understood to be the only God. According to Isaiah here, the Messiah would not simply be sent from God, he would himself be God; and John's Gospel shows the accuracy of this aspect of Isaiah's prophetic name.

Isaiah's name also shows that the Messiah will be the people's

Eternal-Father. Abraham had been chosen by God to be the human head and father of the natural Israel. The Messiah was to be the eternal Head and Father of the true Israel, and Matthew introduces Jesus as 'son of Abraham' and heir of Abraham's Genesis 17 covenant with God.

Finally, Isaiah says that the Messiah will also be the Prince-of-Peace. He will come and fight a decisive battle which will provide peace with God and peace with all humanity. This foreshadows Jesus as the one who comes to provide peace with God through his death on the cross.

Ezekiel's vision

The prophet Ezekiel was given a most remarkable series of visions when the hand of *Yahweh* came upon him by the River Chebar. In the first vision he saw a stormy wind blowing from the north (Ezek 1:4–28). The wind brought a great cloud with flashing fire and brilliant light. In the middle of the fire Ezekiel saw an even greater brilliance, and, in the middle of the brilliance, four living creatures.

The four living creatures were of human form, but the sight of them was like the glory of God. Each one had four faces, four hands and four wings, and they only went where the Spirit urged them. It is their four faces which are significant: 'As to the appearance of their faces, all four had a human face, and a lion's face to the right, and all four had a bull's face to the left, and all four had an eagle's face' (Ezek 1:10).

For second- and third-century theologians this vision was the clinching and most important fourfold foreshadowing of the four Gospels. They were convinced that these four living creatures pointed to four different aspects of the person and ministry of Jesus. At first they disagreed about which creature represented which Gospel, but by the fifth century there was much agreement that the lion, the king of the beasts and source of universal fear and respect, represented the royal side of Jesus stressed by Matthew; that the bull or ox, the hard-working beast who was cruelly slaughtered as soon as its useful service was over, was an exquisite picture of the suffering servant emphasised by Mark; that the face of a man represented Luke's perfect example of humanity for all races and all ages; and that the eagle, the creature which soars in the sky where God was thought to live, represented the living Word which came down from heaven to earth.

Ezekiel's vision

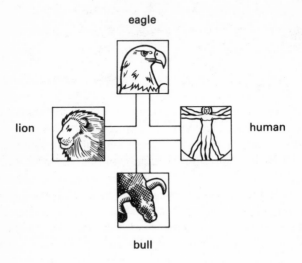

eagle

lion   human

bull

Some 800 years after Ezekiel, these four creatures were seen again, by John while he was a prisoner on Patmos.

> In front of the throne was a sea as transparent as crystal. In the middle of the throne and around it, were four living creatures all studded with eyes, in front and behind. The first living creature was like a lion, the second like a bull, the third living creature had a human face, and the fourth living creature was like a flying eagle (Rev 4:6–7).

The order given to the four creatures in John's vision is the order that the early church leaders adopted for the four Gospels—Matthew, Mark, Luke, then John. Some of them believed that the creatures represented the four Gospels, while others thought that they represented the four writers or evangelists.

Early illustrated copies of the Gospels were decorated with pictures of the living creatures; in later years the four creatures were included in stained glass windows and carved in wood or stone on the four corners of many pulpits to remind preacher and people of the fourfold gospel; and virtually all lecterns, where the word of God was chained and read, were shaped into the form of a flying eagle. Never has so little been made of the fourfold principle as in the last hundred years.

Applying the principle

The fourfold principle was not included in the Old Testament by accident, nor to appeal to human curiosity. It is there to point towards—to foreshadow—the fourfold nature of Jesus, and to remind believers to worship God in his fourfold nature.

There is only one God in heaven, but he reveals himself in the Old Testament in four main ways. Each aspect of God should be experienced and adored, but—sadly—many Christians limit their worship because they favour one aspect or another. Some Old Testament characters only worshipped one side of God's nature (for example: David, *Yahweh Sabaoth*; Daniel, *El Elyon*; and Jacob, *El Shaddai*). But Christians today can know all four aspects, and should worship and proclaim each aspect.

Though the name 'Lord of Hosts' is rarely used today, it is the name which lies behind the 'power' concept that so many believers have of their God. Yet this is only one side of God. Those believers who are preoccupied with spiritual warfare, with power and authority, with kingdom concepts, with the importance of strong leadership, with singing hymns full of military symbolism, and with worshipping an all-powerful masculine God, would do well to acknowledge that they are focusing too much on *Yahweh Sabaoth*.

Many Christians worship God as Saviour from death and sin without going on to celebrate him as protector in the richer, fuller sense of *El Elyon,* the Most High. All Christians need to make more room for the theme of God's protection and to give more time in worship to celebrating this side of his nature.

Some believers are devoted to *El Shaddai's* interests of caring for the weak and providing for their needs. This side of God should never be ignored, but neither should it be the only face of God that is served and adored.

God is still known and worshipped as 'the Holy One'. And there are some Christians who, convinced that God is primarily *El Qodesh*, neglect his other sides, and become over-interested in matters like mystical worship, spiritual disciplines, holy sacraments and sexual purity. A better balance in their thinking would mean that their worship and preaching more accurately reflected God's nature.

The Tabernacle decorations and bloody sacrifices are further reminders of the importance of fourfold worship, as are the four cups drunk at Passover and the four candlesticks lit at Tabernacles. God's law meant that the Jews were not allowed to favour one particular offering; they had to offer the blood sacrifice appropriate for each occasion. As a result, during any one year they offered a balance of all four. So, too, Christian worship through the year should focus on all sides of God's nature.

The Holy Spirit inspired writers to prepare the way for the Messiah with four offices, four creatures, four 'beholds' and Isaiah's prophetic fourfold name. Taken together, these suggest that the Messiah will be one person who is simultaneously powerful king, protecting servant, providing human, and perfect God; that he will be like a lion, a bull, a human, and an eagle; and that he will be a king, a priest, an ordinary man, and a prophet. So Christians today should understand and appreciate Jesus in the fullness of his nature; they should worship him with fourfold variety; and they should boldly and clearly proclaim his full glory to all humankind. Jesus is always one person, but he reveals himself to people in four distinctive ways, and he is to be worshipped for all eternity in precisely these four different ways.

8

The Fourfold Jesus

The Holy Spirit came to earth to lead people into complete truth. As part of that process, he inspired different authors and editors to research, write, preserve, select and arrange material about the earthly life of Jesus; and they shaped four different Gospels with their four distinctive themes and emphases.

The writers

The writers were real people, and if (though most scholars doubt this) they were the traditionally designated authors, they were remarkably well suited to their particular viewpoint.

If Matthew the tax-collector wrote the first Gospel, he was well able to write about righteousness, authority and judgement. In the service of either Caesar or Herod he would almost certainly have been used to flouting his legal authority by charging more in taxes than was officially demanded. As one of Jesus' twelve apostles he would have had to learn a new obedience to God and human authorities, a new respect for laws and for other people, and a new and higher standard of upright behaviour. Perhaps he was also deeply aware that God's judgement on his life had been superseded by mercy, forgiveness and acceptance.

It is possible that the writer of the second Gospel was a servant at the Last Supper, for only he reports on a young man who followed Jesus to Gethsemane wearing nothing but a linen cloth, and, when caught, 'left the cloth in their hands and ran away naked' (Mk 14:52). If that was Mark, he may also have been the Mark who assisted Paul and Barnabas on their first missionary journey. As such, he would have had to get things done while the leaders were talking, and would have experienced the self-effacing role of a servant. Later on, when he found the going too difficult, he suffered rejection under Paul's impatience. Perhaps there was nobody better suited for the task of writing the Gospel of the suffering servant of God.

The four writers?

beloved disciple

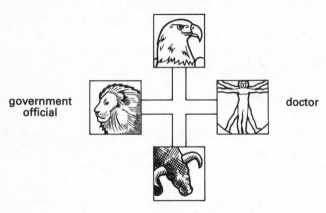

government official   doctor

apostles' servant

Most scholars believe that Luke wrote the third Gospel as well as the book of Acts. He was a Gentile doctor, probably from Greece; and it is not surprising that such a man, with all his insights into human nature, was inspired by the Spirit to write the humanitarian Gospel.

Tradition names John, the son of Zebedee and probably a cousin of Jesus, as principal author of the fourth Gospel. He describes himself as the disciple whom Jesus loved, into whose care Jesus entrusted his mother. As one of the inner three disciples, John was especially close to Jesus and would have gained a deep understanding of Jesus as the Son of God.

The themes

As has been shown, Matthew's Gospel focuses on Jesus as king, and it has much unique teaching, as in the Sermon on the Mount. The key word in Matthew is 'righteousness'. The Gospel is greatly concerned with the kingdom of heaven and what it is like; with authority and who has a right to exercise it; and with judgement and the second coming of Jesus as judge. It is the most Jewish of the Gospels, containing far more quotations from the Old Testament than any other Gospel, and is concerned to show how the ancient prophecies are fulfilled. Only this Gospel reports Jesus' claim that all authority in heaven and on earth has been given to him.

Mark, by contrast, is a Gospel of few words. It is about action, not teaching, and its emphases are Jesus as God's servant, human service and self-sacrifice. Its special word is 'immediately'. And only in Mark is Jesus shown to be still serving on earth after his ascension.

Luke's concerns are humanitarian, Gentile rather than Jewish. The writer is interested in the poor and needy, and in women and tax-collectors. He records parables about 'a certain man who . . .'; and he selects material to show Jesus' perfect humanity, to underline the importance of generosity and to stress the help of the Holy Spirit. The key phrases are 'follow me' and 'filled with the Holy Spirit'. Only Luke points out that Jesus forgives enemies and befriends sinners while dying on the cross.

John's main theme is the glorious Son of God who shows the world what the Father is like. Jesus' divinity is attested by specially selected miracles, by claims to oneness with the Father, and by great sayings introduced with an emphatic 'I am'. This Gospel's key words are 'life', 'belief', 'light', 'truth', 'love' and 'glory'; and only John mentions the term 'new birth'.

The Bible consists of sixty-six books which were written or compiled by many different writers at widely different moments in history. Taken together, these books make up God's final written word to humankind; and taken separately, each one has its distinctive part to play in God's total revelation of himself.

The four Gospels are no exception. There are four because it seems to have pleased the Spirit to reveal Jesus primarily as king, servant, man, and God; and, whether consciously or unconsciously, each of the Gospel writers concentrated in their unique material on one of these themes. Together they write one gospel about one person, yet separately they distinguish different, though overlapping, aspects of his character and work.

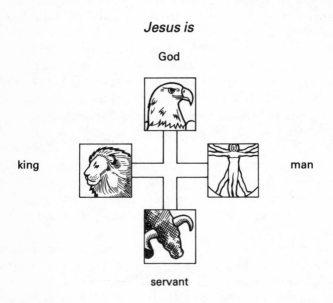

Jesus is

God

king   man

servant

Only Jesus can at the same time be king, servant, man and God. And only Jesus could accomplish simultaneously four distinctive things on the cross. But while he is always one person and his work on the cross is one complete achievement, a Christian's understanding is impoverished when Jesus is viewed and worshipped from only one angle. Just as light needs to pass through a prism before its component colours can be visible, so

Jesus can only be fully appreciated when he is seen with fourfold vision.

The Trinity

Some people who wonder why there are four Gospels think that it would make more sense if there were three, because there are three members of the Holy Trinity. But they miss the point that God reveals himself in four ways through the Trinity, for he shows himself as Father, as Son, as Spirit, and as Three-in-One— which is perhaps why he showed himself in the Tabernacle as three different colours on the fine linen backcloth. The mystery of the Trinity is not only that God expresses himself as three Persons, but also that he reveals himself as one indivisible being who eternally exists in a union of perfect love.

Trinitarian emphasis

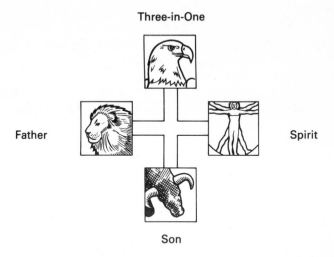

Three-in-One

Father

Spirit

Son

If Jesus' revelation of God is perfect, he must show the Father, and show the Son, and show the Spirit, and show the Three-in-One Trinity, in their relationships and relevance to humankind.

Obviously there is considerable overlap, but Matthew seems to concentrate on the 'Father' aspects of God. He shows the Father working his purpose out throughout history, ruling his earthly family, establishing his heavenly kingdom on earth, and, though rejected, soon to come as king and judge in visible triumph.

Mark focuses on the 'Son' aspects of God, revealing the executive functions of sonship within the Godhead. He shows the Son coming to carry out the family purpose by serving men and dying in their place on the cross: it is God at work for man.

The Spirit applies what the Father has directed and the Son has achieved, so Luke focuses on the 'Holy Spirit' aspects of God: on God at work in man. He stresses the importance of perseverance and of getting alongside people; and only he describes ordinary men and women being filled with the Holy Spirit.

John's Gospel reveals the 'Trinity' aspects of God. He shows that the Father and the Son and the Spirit are eternally one, and that they co-operate together in the work of passing on eternal life, light and truth, and in adopting a new member of the divine family.

Four genealogies

Sometimes the fourfold principle can be seen clearly in the way the Holy Spirit inspired one event to be treated in four different ways by the four Gospel writers. As has been shown, Jesus' ancestry is presented quite distinctively by Matthew, Mark, Luke and John, and each way is typical of that writer's particular view.

Matthew starts with the two foundation figures of Israel: with the patriarch Abraham, from whom the whole nation was descended, and with David, the nation's greatest king. He shows how Joseph, Jesus' official father, is from the royal tribe of Judah in direct line from these great men of the past, and how, therefore, even on a human level Jesus is qualified to be king of Israel.

Mark offers no genealogy, for his is a Gospel about service, and servants are not important because of their origin, but because of the quality of their service.

Luke places his genealogy after Jesus' baptism, to stress his identification with ordinary people, and gives what is sometimes regarded as Mary's family tree. In addition to some differences from Matthew's names, Luke does not trace his genealogy forwards through history from the great Jewish figures of the past, but backwards—as ordinary people do. By going back to Adam and God, Luke shows Jesus' universal kinship with all humankind.

Even though he was, possibly, better placed to know the stories than the other three writers, John ignores Jesus' human origins. Instead, he records Jesus' heavenly genealogy and the eternal relationship of the Word with God, as befits the Gospel of Jesus as divine Son of God.

Genealogies

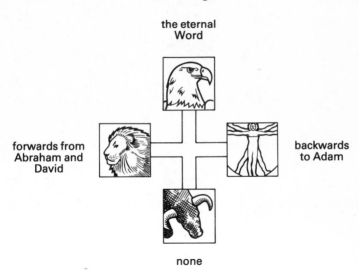

the eternal
Word

forwards from
Abraham and
David

backwards
to Adam

The fourfold fish

Sometimes the fourfold principle can be seen outside the Scriptures in the way the Holy Spirit inspired believers to express their commitment to Jesus and each other. For example, when early believers were driven underground they used the symbol of a fish to recognise each other.

This was particularly appropriate because the Greek word for fish, *ichthus*, is made up of letters which stand for a fourfold description of Jesus: *I* (*Iesous*— Jesus), *Ch* (*Christos*—Christ), *Th U* (*Theou Uios*—God's Son), *S* (*Soter*—Saviour). This is a highly biblical description, and its constant use in the Roman catacombs reminded the persecuted believers that they followed a fourfold leader: one who was known by the name Jesus; who was the Christ, the anointed man; who was the glorious Son of God; and who had saved them from their sins.

The fourfold name

God's Son

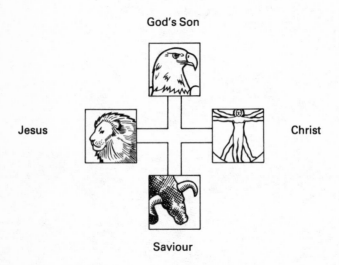

Jesus   Christ

Saviour

Angels and treasure

Sometimes the fourfold principle can be seen in incidents which are reported in only one Gospel. Although each Gospel does have distinctive themes, within every Gospel there are particular passages which hint at Jesus' fourfold nature. One instance is when an angel spoke to the shepherds, and said, 'Today in the town of David a Saviour has been born to you; he is Christ the Lord' (Lk 2:11).

The city of David was Bethlehem. Over seven hundred years

earlier, Micah had prophesied that from Bethlehem 'will come for me a future ruler of Israel whose origins go back to the distant past' (Mic 5:2). So the baby was qualified by his place of birth to be the long-awaited king.

But the angel makes it plain that the baby is not only a king, he is also a Saviour, one who has come to serve and give his life as a ransom for many; he is the Christ, the anointed man; and he is the Lord, worthy to be called by the jealously guarded name of God.

The good news of great joy

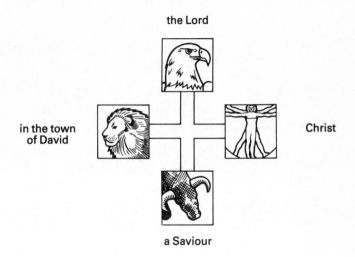

the Lord

in the town of David

Christ

a Saviour

Another example of the fourfold principle within one Gospel is the visit of the Wise Men. Matthew 2:9–12 shows that they expressed their worship of the newborn child in a variety of ways.

People often think that just after Jesus was born three kings brought three types of presents. But all that can be said with certainty is that an unknown number of wise men or astrologers brought treasure chests from their country in the East. On arrival, they 'fell down and worshipped him. Then, opening their treasures, they offered him gifts, gold and frankincense and myrrh' (Mt 2:11, RSV).

The men had been convinced in advance that the infant was a king, so they had brought with them gifts which were worthy of his royal status. Most people think that these gifts were the gold, frankincense and myrrh, but frankincense and myrrh would have been strange gifts to give to a king. Matthew does not list everything that was in their treasure chests, and the Greek is ambiguous: it is not clear whether the word 'gifts' supplements or summarises the gold, frankincense and myrrh. It is possible that, having seen the child, the Wise Men selected other presents from their treasures which, in addition to their gifts for a king, prophetically pointed to the other three sides of Jesus' nature.

The Wise Men's treasures

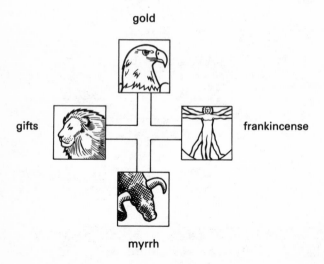

gold

gifts

frankincense

myrrh

The carol 'We three kings' has popularised many assumptions about the men: from Matthew's viewpoint it would have been very appropriate if the Wise Men really had been kings, but he does not say so. As well as its assumptions about the number and status of the men, the carol also inaccurately describes the symbolism behind their presents.

They chose gold, then the most valuable substance on earth. It had been used in the Tabernacle to represent God's heavenly glory and his presence on earth; and its use by the astrologers indicated that the child would bring God's glory to earth. They also picked out sweet frankincense to show that the child was a man whose life would ascend, like the wholly-burnt offerings, as sweet-smelling incense to God. And they were inspired to select bitter myrrh, which is universally acknowledged as a symbol of suffering, thus suggesting that the child would suffer in life and die a terrible death.

Jesus' miracles

Sometimes the fourfold principle can be seen in an overview of one aspect of Jesus' life, for example, the miracles. The four Gospels all report a variety of miracles, so no one Gospel has a monopoly of one type of miracle. However, one obvious way of grouping the miracles reflects the fourfold principle and points forward towards their culmination in the great miracle of the cross.

Four types of miracle

nature (feeding and stilling)

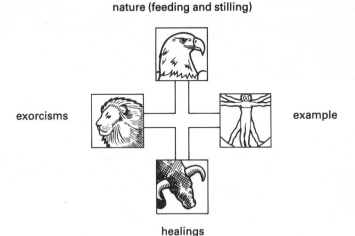

exorcisms   example

healings

Jesus' miracles can be divided into three main kinds—exorcisms, healings and nature miracles (feedings and stillings). The exorcisms demonstrate Jesus' authority over evil spirits, and point forward to Jesus' final victory over Satan on the cross. The healings demonstrate Jesus' calling to cure all that is wrong in men and women (the Greek verb *sozo*, 'to save', includes the idea of healing or saving from sickness), and point towards the way in which Jesus comprehensively deals with sin and all its effects on the cross. The feeding and stilling miracles demonstrate the ability of the Son of God to offer peace and to give life and satisfaction to all who come to him, and point forward to their fulfilment in the cross when Jesus wins eternal life for humankind.

That leaves the great miracle of a life wholly without sin and positively perfect in every respect, a life of complete obedience to the Father, even to death on a cross.

Moreover, each individual miracle can be examined from the four different viewpoints. Some believers today focus on Jesus' authority. They emphasise the way he instantly brings freedom, wholeness or food, and try themselves to minister in an equally impressive way.

Other Christians study the small details of his miraculous service—his words, looks, gestures and touches—and seek to imitate them in the hope that by doing so they will share his effectiveness.

More people look at the way Jesus cares for sufferers and shows his deep compassion and sympathy for their plight, and they aim to care for the needy with similar devotion.

And a few believers stare at a miracle and see God alone at work, and his glory as the most important outcome. Their response is usually either prayer or despair.

It is most important that every miracle, whether in the Gospels, in history or today, should be seen from all these four viewpoints so that an unbalanced response may be avoided.

Jesus' transport

Sometimes the fourfold principle can be seen in an overview of

Jesus' life which looks beyond the four Gospels, as with Jesus' means of transport.

Jesus was born in Bethlehem, and some of his ministry took place in and around Judaea, but the larger part of his life was spent in the region sixty or so miles to the north, in Nazareth, around the sea of Galilee, and right up to Caesarea Philippi in the far north. Jesus identified with the common people and travelled as they travelled, mostly on foot and, where appropriate, in a boat. Clearly he spent a great deal of time walking from village to village, and this would have marked him out as a very ordinary man.

Four modes of transport

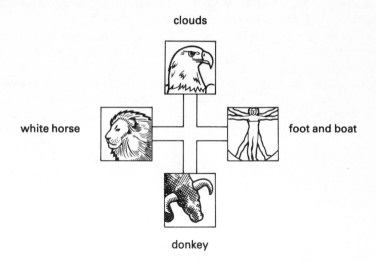

clouds

white horse

foot and boat

donkey

When Jesus visited Jerusalem, he almost always entered the city on foot, but the Bible records one occasion that was different. On the Sunday before Passover Jesus borrowed a donkey—a very lowly animal, a servant-beast of burden which throughout history has often been scandalously maltreated by its owners. Jesus' choice of a donkey for his entry into Jerusalem showed that on that occasion the Saviour had not come to overthrow the

Romans, but in humility and peace to give his life for all. The people's cry 'Hosanna' (which means 'save now') had a deeper and more wonderful meaning than the cheering crowds suspected.

On Palm Sunday the people hoped that Jesus would be a king. Revelation 19:11–16 shows that one day he will be 'King of kings and Lord of lords', and that he will ride out on a white horse at the head of the armies of heaven to rule unbelievers and to tread out the wine of God's retribution. Revelation 6:2 and (possibly) Zechariah 6:1–8 also hint that the one who once rode on a donkey will one day ride on a horse to rule and to execute God's judgement.

The first three Gospels record Jesus foretelling his fourth and final mode of transport: 'They will see the Son of man coming in a cloud with power and great glory' (Lk 21:27). This recalls Daniel 7 where Daniel dreams of the satanic counterfeit of Jesus' fourfold nature. In the end the four beasts were totally destroyed and only the one who rides on the clouds is served for ever:

> Before me was one like a son of man, coming with the clouds of heaven. He approached the Ancient of Days and was led into his presence. He was given authority, glory and sovereign power; all peoples, nations and men of every language worshipped him. His dominion is an everlasting dominion that will not pass away, and his kingdom is one that will never be destroyed (Dan 7:13–14, NIV).

Jesus' baptism

As has been seen, the four accounts of Jesus' baptism differ from each other. However, they are sufficiently similar to allow an examination of an overview of the baptism. This reveals that several examples of the fourfold principle run through the accounts.

Jesus came to the Jordan to obey the Father and to submit to every ordinance of man for the Father's sake; after obeying, he went forward in authority to rule over Satan.

But Jesus also came to the Jordan willing to take a lowly position and to accept ministry from his cousin. Then he went away— to be looked after by angels, to be with wild animals, and to prepare for service.

Jesus comes to the Jordan

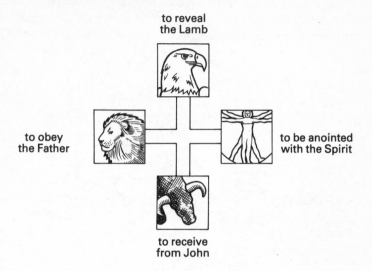

to reveal
the Lamb

to obey
the Father

to be anointed
with the Spirit

to receive
from John

Jesus also came to the Jordan to be anointed with the Spirit. He left behind his family, friends, job, security and possessions, and he put himself unconditionally at the disposal of the Father. Then, after his anointing, he followed the Spirit into the desert, ready to lead men and women and to call them to follow him.

And Jesus also came to the Jordan as the Lamb, to show people what God is like, and as the Lamb he went down into the water to symbolise death, and came up out of the water to begin offering new life to humanity.

The baptism itself has four distinct phases. Jesus went down into the water and was submerged, or had water poured over him, to symbolise the end of his old life; he rose up out of the water to begin a new life; he stood praying; the heavens opened and the Spirit descended upon him.

This fourfold sequence of death, resurrection, prayer and empowering was lived out in Jesus' daily experience. He died daily to self; he lived the victorious risen life; he prepared for everything in prayer; and he was reassured and empowered by the

Spirit for every aspect of his ministry. Historically, this sequence was then fulfilled by Jesus' death; by his resurrection; by his prayers for his disciples and for the Spirit to come; and by the outpouring of the Spirit at Pentecost.

At Jesus' baptism

he stands praying

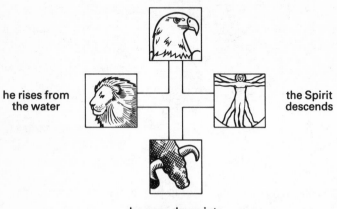

he rises from the water   **the Spirit descends**

he goes down into the water

Each of these four phases of the baptism sequence can itself be examined in the light of the four main faces of Jesus so that a full and balanced picture of baptism and baptised living is seen. Usually this does not happen. Some Christians tend to look at Jesus' life more from the kingly viewpoint, while others unconsciously prefer one of the other three viewpoints. As a result, when believers think or speak about an incident like Jesus' baptism, they receive only the insights provided by their limited viewpoint. The fourfold principle helps believers to look beyond their natural viewpoint to see and appreciate other aspects of truth and so possess and proclaim a fuller and more balanced understanding of Jesus' person and ministry.

Fourfold vision enables Jesus' descent into the water to be viewed, from the kingly side, as a symbol of judgement and

	his going into the water signifies:	his rising from the water signifies:	his prayers could be for:	the descent of the Spirit signifies:
kingly view	judgement, repentance	his authority	his obedience to the Father	power to face Satan
serving view	his bearing the sins of others	his cleanliness	his sacrifice to be effective	power to serve and heal
human view	everything dedicated to God	his public ministry	his perfection and perseverance	a gift of vital assurance
divine view	the grain of wheat dies	reborn in glory	fruitfulness and God's glory	ready to display life, light, glory and love

repentance; from the serving side, as a symbolic bearing of the sins of the world; from the human side, as a dedication of everything to God; and from the divine side, both as a grain of wheat going into the ground and as a woman travailing in childbirth.

His coming out of the water can be seen as a symbol of his resurrection authority; as a symbol of his cleanliness; as an indication that the time for secrecy is over and everything will now be in public; and as a raising in glory, a birth, and a new shoot which will reproduce itself many times.

Jesus could be praying for his mind, body and spirit to be entirely under God's authority; for his sacrifice to be effective in his future followers' lives; for himself, that he will live his life faultlessly and accomplish everything that God has purposed for him; and for God to glorify himself and make the Son fruitful.

The pouring out of the Spirit can be understood as an empowering with authority for his confrontation with evil spirits and disease; as an equipping for his dove-like sacrifice and service; as a gift of vital assurance; and as the resource for radiating God's glory, light, life and love.

This type of analysis can helpfully be applied to many other parts of Jesus' life and ministry.

Jesus' purpose

The fourfold principle helps Christians to grasp why Jesus came into the world. The Gospels suggest four main reasons for his coming, and these must all be understood for a balanced view of the incarnation.

First of all, Jesus came to break the power of evil and death. The fallen angel Lucifer had taken authority on earth and the whole world was under his sway. Jesus came into the world to establish the kingdom of heaven, to disarm the evil powers of darkness, to make a public spectacle of them, and to triumph over them by the cross. He came to preach a gospel of repentance, to teach his followers the consequence of disobedience, and to give them clear guidelines for behaviour.

Secondly, Jesus came to seek and to save the lost. He came to save needy people who were powerless to save themselves. At great personal sacrifice, he came to make atonement for the sins of all humanity, to act as a substitute for each member of humankind and to bear the wrath of God against sin.

Thirdly, Jesus came to demonstrate a life of perfect consecration; to be the pattern and example for men and women of all ages and all races. In his daily death to self and the desires of the flesh, and in his death on the cross, he came to show human beings how they should live and die.

And, fourthly, Jesus came to show what God is like. He came to reveal the glorious Father. He came as God's living Word, as a unique and complete revelation of the invisible God, to reproduce the divine nature in humankind.

Why did he come?

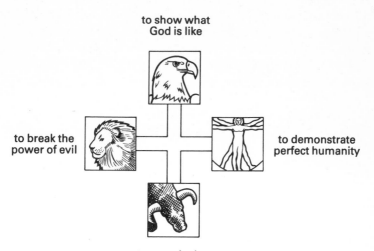

to show what
God is like

to break the
power of evil

to demonstrate
perfect humanity

to save the lost

It is a great tragedy that the church has seldom embraced all these four insights in balance, for all are biblical and all are true. Catholics, for example, have tended to major on Matthew's authoritarian viewpoint, as do the New Churches. Evangelicals have always emphasised Mark's atoning viewpoint. Liberals have stressed Luke's human viewpoint. Meanwhile, the Orthodox Churches—and, more recently, charismatics—have focused on the glories of John's heavenly emphases.

The fourfold principle should encourage Christians to appreciate the viewpoint of other Christian traditions, and to realise that—like each of the four Gospels—they need to stand with those whose Christian viewpoints differ from their own, so that the world can know the complete truth about Jesus.

9

The Fourfold Gospel

There may be four Gospels, but there is only one gospel, which can helpfully be presented in four different ways. If Christian evangelism is to be both accurate and effective, each aspect of every side of the one gospel should be both understood and proclaimed.

The first consequences of sin

Jesus came into the world to reverse the four terrible consequences of the fall of humankind in the Garden of Eden; he came to remedy the creature's rebellion against the Creator which is reported in Genesis 3.

First, when Adam and Eve sinned, humanity was bound by and to Satan. They lost the glorious freedom of the children of God because they had rejected the authority of God and had accepted that of the devil. From that time on, the world was under the control of the Evil One.

Secondly, as a result of their sin, humanity became guilty. It was under God's wrath. This led to the punishment in this life, of increased suffering in childbirth and increased sweat in work, and, in the life to come, of hell.

Thirdly, people became alienated from each other because of their embarrassment and shame at their shortcomings. Adam and Eve's futile attempt to cover their nakedness with leaves and to hide behind trees was because they were ashamed to face God.

They took their shame with them when they left the garden, and it went on to affect their relationships with other people. Sin always ultimately results in a sense of shame, and attempts to cover up, or to hide, fail to deal with that sense of shame.

Fourthly, the wages of the first sin was death. Adam and Eve forfeited the privilege of close fellowship with God which is eternal life. They had ignored God's warning and had eaten from the tree of the knowledge of good and evil, so an angel was posted at the entrance of the garden to prevent them from eating the fruit of the tree of life.

The results of the fall

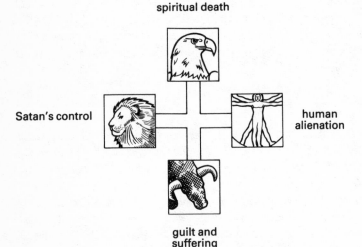

spiritual death

Satan's control

human alienation

guilt and suffering

Jesus, then, came to bring humanity freedom from Satan, forgiveness from sin, unashamed friendship with each other, and eternal life and sustenance from himself. Any presentation of the gospel which focuses too much on one of these consequences and remedies, or which ignores one of them, is not a proclamation of the full gospel.

The final consequences of sin

It is a sobering thought that many of the most solemn biblical descriptions of hell come from the lips of Jesus. Hell is, quite naturally, not a popular topic, but there is little integrity in reading and preaching those scriptural passages which are pleasant and comforting, and in ignoring those that are not.

People were created to find perfect freedom in God's service by submitting to God's will and controlling human passions. Experience teaches that unbridled indulgence, whether in money, sex, knowledge, or anything else, leads to unhappiness, disease or even death. Human licence always turns out to be the opposite of true liberty. So total and eternal enslavement to self-will is the final consequence of persisting in rebellion against Jesus' claim to be the rightful ruler of every life. Those who refuse to enter Jesus' kingdom of heaven while they are on earth, will find that it is too late in the after-life.

Everybody has broken at least one of God's laws and has injured other people in one way or another. And this means that everybody has a natural desire to make amends. But experience shows that no matter how many good deeds are done, they never make up for the few bad things: a burglar cannot plead in court that many more days have been lived honestly than have been given over to robbery. So the final result of breaking God's laws and not relying on Christ's reparation sacrifice is punishment and hellish imprisonment which continues for ever and from which there is neither escape nor relief.

There is only one ground on which the righteous God can forgive sin, and that is the death of Jesus in the sinner's place; and there is only one way in which that forgiveness can be applied to an individual's record, and that is by personal reliance on Jesus' death alone. Without such cleansing, guilt remains—and remains eternally: the torture of clearly seeing the evil done and the good not done must be hell indeed. There will be no peace for the wicked, or for those who have confidently supposed themselves to be righteous but are not.

Jesus is the embodiment of all that is good: to exclude him, ultimately means excluding all that is good. People are becoming in this life what they will be like for eternity, and the final consequence of refusing to follow the example of Christ in this life is an eternal existence without his love, joy, peace, patience, kindness, goodness, faithfulness, gentleness and self-control. People who do not embrace and emulate Jesus' life now will not be worth knowing hereafter. Only Jesus and his friends will be characterised by the fruit of God's Spirit; only they will be what all people should be. And they will not be found, for a great chasm will have been fixed for ever.

Finally, the person who will not have the love of God now will be left with its opposite—loneliness and separation. Only eternal death will remain for those who will not have eternal life now. Only everlasting darkness will exist for those who will not come to the Light of the world now. And those who will not believe in the truth on earth will only experience the results of deception in the hereafter. As Isaiah prophesied so long ago, 'there will be no dawn for them' (8:20).

The final results of sin

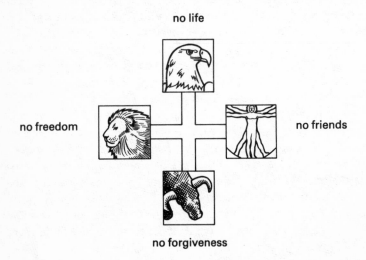

no life

no freedom

no friends

no forgiveness

The final consequences of sin are grim, and seem especially so for those many people who live fairly decent, law-abiding lives. But such people also existed in Jesus' day, and he had no hesitation in clearly stating: 'The road that leads to destruction is wide and spacious, and many take it' (Mt 7:13), and 'they will go away to eternal punishment, and the upright to eternal life' (Mt 25:46).

The human condition and God's response

In the light of these consequences, it is possible to give a simplified fourfold summary of the one gospel. This summary is an accurate and complete picture of today's human condition and clearly shows the response that God has made to remedy that condition. It is important that contemporary evangelism should address all four of these basic problems and describe God's complete response in Jesus.

By their very human nature, all people alive today are in the grip of the world, the flesh and the devil. No matter how hard they

God sent Jesus to be

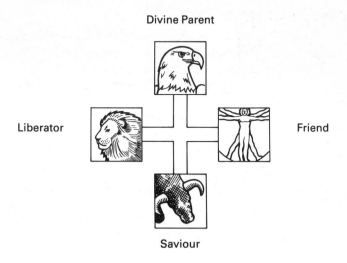

Divine Parent

Liberator

Friend

Saviour

try, they cannot break completely free from that grip. So God has sent Jesus as Liberator to break that bondage and to offer freedom to everybody.

By nature all people are guilty before God because of their sin. No matter what they do they cannot escape from their burden of guilt. So Jesus has willingly come as Saviour to experience God's anger in place of each individual sinner, and to make forgiveness available to all.

By nature, people are sometimes ashamed and embarrassed in front of each other. No matter what help they receive, they can still find it hard to relate to other people because of something which is fundamentally wrong. So Jesus has come as Friend to bring complete understanding and perfect sympathy for each person's difficulties, and to be the comforter, companion, and counsellor whom everyone needs.

And all people are spiritually dead. People who are dead can never resuscitate themselves. So Jesus has come as divine parent to strain for the heavenly birth of each member of humanity and to make eternal life freely available for all.

Human need and God's provision

Evangelists need to preach the gospel from all sorts of different angles, so it is helpful to look at humanity from a slightly different perspective, summarise the state of humankind, see its four basic needs and note that God has perfectly met all these needs in the fourfold Jesus.

Humankind exists in a basic state of rebellion against God, and every individual member needs to be brought into obedience to God. So God has provided Jesus as the ruler and king to whom people must submit.

Every person alive has committed some sins and needs a bloody sacrifice to deal with that sin. So God has provided Jesus as the sacrifice who removes sin.

Society experiences disunity and fragmentation, and its members need to become whole, integrated with other people, able to relate easily with other individuals, classes and races. So God has provided Jesus as the example of wholeness, social integration and perfect inter-personal relationships.

And every individual member of humanity is spiritually dead, needing to receive life, light, truth and love from God. So God has provided Jesus as the source of these eternal qualities.

People today live in

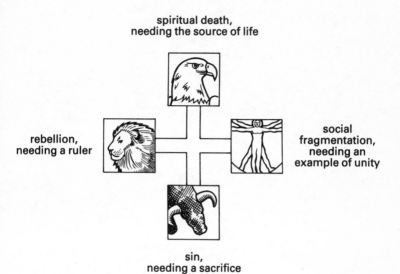

spiritual death,
needing the source of life

rebellion,
needing a ruler

social
fragmentation,
needing an
example of unity

sin,
needing a sacrifice

Why Jesus died

When believers preach the gospel they usually need to explain why Jesus died. Some people look at the gospel from only one viewpoint and ask why God could not have announced forgiveness like the father of the prodigal son. They want mercy without justice, love without righteousness: the benefits of the cross without any of the agony. But fourfold vision enables believers to appreciate that Jesus died for four great complementary reasons.

Jesus died to rescue humankind from Satan's grip. He descended to the depths of hell, wrenched the keys of death away from Satan so that nobody need any longer be in his sway, and returned in triumph. Jesus died and rose again as the victor who destroys even Satan's last card, death. By his death, he establishes the kingdom of God, sets people free, and eternally fulfils every aspect of the Old Testament reparation offering.

Jesus died as

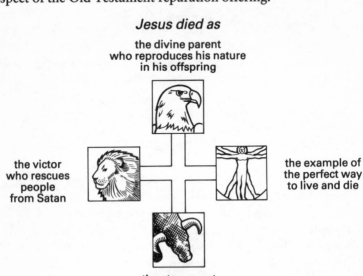

the divine parent
who reproduces his nature
in his offspring

the victor
who rescues
people
from Satan

the example of
the perfect way
to live and die

the atonement
who delivers people
from sin

Jesus also died to make atonement for the sin of humanity. On the cross he appeased God's wrath and delivered humankind from sin. He did this by voluntarily accepting the blame, enduring the agony of separation from the Father, taking the faults of many on himself, and winning eternal redemption. So Jesus died to bring forgiveness, and to fulfil permanently every aspect of the Old Testament sin offering and all the Old Testament prophecies that point to substitutionary death by God's servant/priest as the only acceptable ground on which God can cleanse and justify a sinner.

Jesus also died to leave an example of the ideal way for a human being to live and die. Even while he suffered Jesus made time to show exemplary human behaviour in asking God to forgive those who tortured him, and in comforting a criminal with the promise that he would be with him in paradise. And when he died he left everything behind and committed his spirit into God's hands. Jesus died to provide for all time an example of perfect obedience, and to fulfil all the details of the Levitical wholly burnt offering.

And, at the same time, Jesus also died on the cross in excruciating pain to struggle and strain for the birth of a new creation. After six hellish hours of spiritual childbirth he was, like the panting deer of Psalm 42:1–2, deeply spiritually thirsty. And as he died in labour he could cry 'I've done it' because, like the servant in Isaiah 53:10, he had seen his offspring. So Jesus went to the cross to travail and give birth to a new creation which would reproduce the divine nature, and to fulfil every aspect of the Old Testament peace offering.

Fourfold evangelism

People start moving along the narrow road that leads to Christian faith for widely differing reasons, but in the main it is possible to classify them into four negative categories and four positive categories.

The unbeliever may be aware that his life is in a mess and needs outside direction, authority, deliverance or new purpose. He hears of Jesus, his authoritative teaching, his victory over evil and his promised return in power, and is attracted to him.

Or the unbeliever may be acutely aware of sin, or of a need for healing or some other help. He hears of the Saviour, his servant ministry, his atoning death on the cross, and is drawn to him.

Or the unbeliever may be experiencing loneliness, or want a special friend to stand alongside him, or feel uncertain and desire some example to follow. He reads stories about Jesus, sees his compassion and sympathetic friendship, and wants to learn more.

Or the unbeliever could be researching religions, and be sincerely searching for the truth about God, life and the universe. He reads the Gospels, or hears a sermon about the Son of God and his unique claims, and is attracted to the Light of the World.

Other people have positive reasons for starting their pilgrimage to belief. The unbeliever may see the victorious life of Jesus lived

People come to Jesus for negative reasons

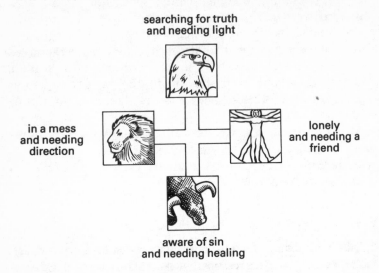

searching for truth
and needing light

in a mess
and needing
direction

lonely
and needing a
friend

aware of sin
and needing healing

out in a friend, read or hear about Jesus' power and authority, and become aware of his own need for Jesus to straighten out his life.

Or the unbeliever may see the effects of a friend's sudden freedom from guilt after becoming a Christian, or read or hear about the Saviour's costly sacrifice, or be impressed by somebody's life of service. As a result, he may be convicted of his own sin and need and turn towards Jesus.

Or the unbeliever may have a devoted Christian friend, or may receive some helpful advice from a Christian, or be somehow drawn to the perfections of Christ. He realises that he needs a friend, companion and example and starts to investigate Jesus.

Or the unbeliever may be greatly moved by Christian worship, or have received a clear spiritual experience, or some revelation of Jesus as God. He feels that this is what he has always needed and begins to join in with the worship.

Of course, these negative and positive categories are not exclusive, but it is important that everyone who attempts to share the

People come to Jesus for positive reasons

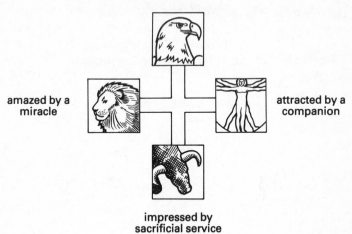

moved by worship

amazed by a miracle

attracted by a companion

impressed by sacrificial service

gospel with others should recognise that people have these different needs, and that specific aspects of Jesus will attract different people at different times.

A believer's evangelistic style is bound to be coloured by the way he or she came to Jesus. If believers restrict themselves to one aspect of the gospel, there will be many people whom they never reach. All believers must therefore try to explore the other complementary sides of evangelism. They need to vary their preaching, speaking, composing and writing to take account of the four main ways in which Christian understanding comes; and they must endeavour to ensure that every new Christian grasps these four aspects of Christian truth, if they are to become balanced and whole.

Old Testament pointers

When some preachers speak about the cross, they like to use Old Testament incidents which foreshadow the gospel message. The problem is that when they select a story they tend to focus on only one or two aspects of the fourfold gospel, and so misrepresent the fullness of the gospel. They need to try to ensure that the passages they pick reflect the main sides of the cross.

The history of Israel is full of incidents which point forwards to the cross and help believers to understand its fourfold meaning. Perhaps the stories of David and Goliath, Moses and Pharaoh, Abraham and Isaac, and Joseph and his brothers, are the clearest illustrations of the four emphases.

Events which point to the cross:

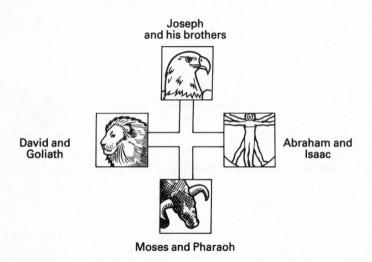

Joseph
and his brothers

David and
Goliath

Abraham and
Isaac

Moses and Pharaoh

The heroic story of David and Goliath (1 Sam 17) is well known, but perhaps not all have deeply understood its significance in relation to the cross. Another enemy, more deadly than Goliath and at the head of an army more powerful and numerous than the Philistines, threatened the people of God. Another despised and unrecognised descendant of Jesse, Jesus of Bethlehem, achieved a final and total victory over the adversary and his minions, completely breaking his power for those who believe. And just as David went triumphantly back to Jerusalem after the battle, leaving the Israelites to press home his victory over the Philistines, so Jesus returned to heaven, leaving his soldiers to press home by faith his victory over a defeated foe.

Earlier in their history Israel had been slaves in Egypt. When, after many warning plagues, Pharaoh had still refused to let God's people go, God told Moses and Aaron that each Israelite household should take a perfect lamb or goat, kill it, and put some of the blood on the outside doorposts and lintels of their houses. That night God killed the firstborn of every human family and of every farm animal in Egypt—but he passed over households whose doorways were marked with blood. Today the judgement of God and the sentence of death hangs over every household in the world, but the perfect Lamb has been sacrificed at Calvary, and those who believe that his blood was shed to achieve their forgiveness will be spared when the most terrible day of judgement finally comes.

The story of Abraham and Isaac on Mount Moriah reflects several aspects of the cross, but prominent among them is Isaac's total trust in his father and his ready submission, however costly, to everything Abraham said and did. The beautiful phrase 'the two of them set out together' (Gen 22:6) anticipates Jesus' complete trust in his Father and his obedience, even to death on a cross.

The history of Joseph contains many things which can illuminate a believer's understanding of Jesus: he makes true claims about himself which arouse jealousy and hatred; he is especially loved by his father; he is rejected by his brothers, but God raises him up to an exalted position; and he lays up vast stores of grain so that he can feed all those who come to him when their human resources have been exhausted. This reflects Jesus' rejection, and his ability and willingness—through death and resurrection—to give life and satisfaction to all those who are humble enough to come to him for sustenance.

The value of the cross

On every continent and throughout all traditions the cross has always been recognised as the symbol of Christianity. Like the four colours of the Old Testament Tabernacle decorations, the four sides of the cross are a perpetual reminder of the fourfold nature of God, Jesus and the gospel.

In years past, the content of hymns, the shape of buildings, the ornaments on altars and walls, the decoration of stained-glass windows, even the design of brooches, have all helpfully emphasised the centrality of the cross. But believers who think about the great value of the cross and claim its importance for their daily lives, would find it even more helpful if they used precise concepts and language.

The value of the cross

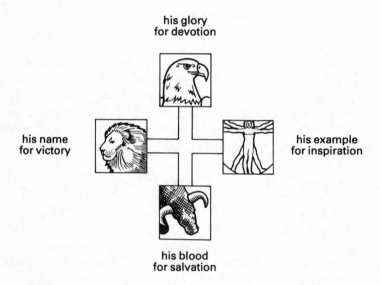

his glory
for devotion

his name
for victory

his example
for inspiration

his blood
for salvation

It is the name of Jesus that enables Christians to share in the victory of the cross, and to act or speak with his supreme authority. It is the blood of Jesus, shed on the cross, that gives believers assurance of acceptance by the God of the whole earth. It is the example of Jesus on the cross that inspires his disciples to live a life marked by forgiveness and ever-increasing consecration. And it is the glory of Jesus, which shone at its brightest on the cross, that is now partially seen in his church and will be fully seen hereafter.

Christians have God's permission to act, speak, pray and protect themselves 'in the name of Jesus'. They can do all these things with his authority, drawing on his victory over the world, the flesh, the devil and death itself. However, the phrase 'the name of Jesus' means the full nature of Jesus. This is partly revealed by the many names and titles in the Bible, including the name 'Jesus'. Together they express his life, his nature, his character, and all the attributes and virtues of God and man in perfect unity and harmony. However, even though Jesus is called 'Trustworthy and True' (Rev 19:11) and 'is known by the name "The Word of God"' (Rev 19:13), and wears the name 'King of kings and Lord of lords' (Rev 19:16) on his cloak and on his thigh, he still has another name which is 'known only to himself' (Rev 19:12).

The shed blood of Jesus is the basis of a Christian's salvation. The 'accuser of the brothers' and the human conscience often bring accusations of sin, but believers who rely on the Saviour's blood can deal with these accusations because they know that their sin and guilt have already been totally removed. It is one of the great glories of the cross that Christians can be sure their sins have been forgiven eternally, and it is possible to hold this assurance without presumption because it depends entirely on the merciful shedding of Jesus' blood and not on anything that a Christian has done or can do.

The example of Jesus' perfect death should inspire all believers to imitate his behaviour, to be filled with the Spirit, to dedicate themselves wholly to God's purposes, to endure suffering with fortitude and patience, to forgive enemies even when they are inflicting great pain, to befriend undeserving criminals, and to die with quiet commitment to God.

And the greatest glory of the cross is that, just as a grain of wheat falls to the ground and dies so that it can multiply itself, so Jesus' death brings about the birth of a vast number of believers who reproduce his divine nature. Those who are part of this glorious new creation can do the same things that Jesus did and show his wonderful glory on the earth.

The benefits of the cross

When Paul wrote to the Corinthian church, he summarised his message of the cross as four great blessings in Jesus which make him worthy of unrestrained eternal thanks and praise: 'It is by him that you exist in Christ Jesus, who for us was made wisdom from God, and saving justice and holiness and redemption. As scripture says: If anyone wants to boast, let him boast of the Lord' (1 Cor 1:30–31).

Jesus has been made his disciples'

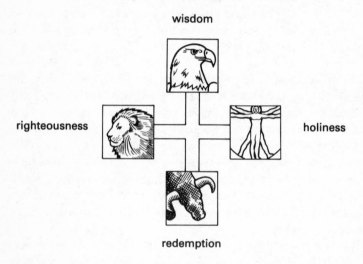

wisdom

righteousness   holiness

redemption

Paul promises that those people who receive Jesus also receive God's wisdom. The Old Testament Wisdom Literature consists of the books of Job, Psalms, Proverbs, Ecclesiastes and the Song of Songs. The first nine chapters of Proverbs are the clearest and most detailed biblical description of God's wisdom. There wisdom is personified and contrasted with her opposite, folly—the refusal to acknowledge or know God. These chapters contain a remarkable series of claims, promises and statements which are remarkably fulfilled and repeated by the Word of God in John's

Gospel, for example, Proverbs 6:23; 7:2; 8:6–8,17,18–21,32–35; 9:5–6.

Paul shows that people who receive Jesus also receive God's saving justice or righteousness. There are two legal reasons why God, the perfectly moral judge, can accept imperfect human believers and declare them to be eternally righteous in his sight. First, it is because their guilt has been removed on the cross, thus making them legally sinless; and secondly, because all the perfections of Jesus have been exchanged for all their imperfections. So when Jesus is received, he brings with him as a gift his own full marks for a righteous entrance into glory.

Whereas from the above judicial viewpoint, a believer is treated as perfectly righteous before God, Paul also shows that believers are, in reality, made increasingly more holy in character and behaviour; for whenever Jesus is received he imparts his perfection—all his virtues and every aspect of his character. This breathtaking miracle of grace is only partially worked out in this life, but it does mean that heaven will be truly heavenly and not just an improvement on earth, for believers will be presented 'glorious, with no speck or wrinkle or anything like that, but holy and faultless' (Eph 5:27).

And Paul also makes it plain that Jesus brings redemption to all who receive him. Redemption implies the idea of buying out or buying back, and it has two strands of meaning in Scripture which are best illustrated by the Israelite deliverance or redemption from Egypt. They were delivered because of the presence of the blood over their doors. This guaranteed that the angel passed over them without executing judgement—and this is redemption from the serving viewpoint. But they were also delivered by the mighty power of God in the crossing of the Red Sea and the destruction of the pursuing Egyptian army—and this is redemption from the kingly viewpoint. To every single believer Jesus brings redemption from guilt through the shedding of blood, and redemption from enslavement to death and the devil through his great victory on the cross.

Jesus' fourfold relationship with a believer

At different times, in different parts of the church, different relationships between Jesus and his followers have been emphasised. For example, within the evangelical tradition during the 1950s and 60s there was great stress on the importance of receiving Jesus as Saviour. Then in the 1970s evangelical believers were pressed to receive him as Lord. And in the 1980s both these relationships were emphasised, as in new hymns like 'The Servant King'.

Jesus is his disciples'

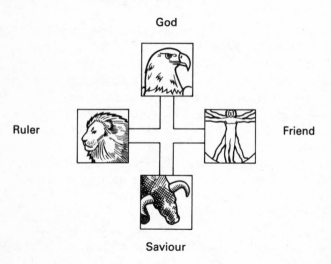

God

Ruler　　　　　　　　　　　　　　　Friend

Saviour

However, Jesus came to have four great relationships with all believers: he came to be ruler, and to be Saviour, and to be Friend and to be God. He is always all of these, but some people focus too much on only one or two of these relationships. All four should be preached and enjoyed with equal enthusiasm, for the gospel cannot be fully preached or responded to if people are only encouraged to receive Jesus as Saviour or obey him as ruler, or if they are only taught to worship him as God without knowing him as Friend.

Believers who know Jesus in only some of these relationships are missing out on the fullness of their inheritance in Christ. Every Christian needs occasional encouragement to check that he or she is obeying Jesus as ruler, and living by the guidelines he laid down in the Sermon on the Mount. Each Christian needs to depend on him as Saviour, and rely absolutely on his sacrifice; to know him as Friend, and be deeply aware of his sympathetic, understanding companionship; to love him as God, and offer him worship in spirit and in truth in every area of life and for every aspect of his nature.

The church's response to Jesus

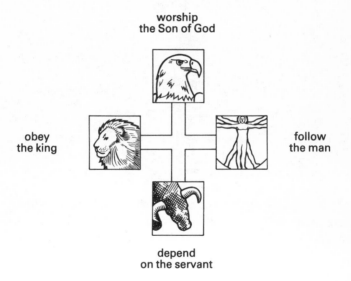

worship
the Son of God

obey
the king

follow
the man

depend
on the servant

In summary, the fourfold response of the church to the gospel should include obeying the king, depending on all that the servant has done, following the man by walking in the Spirit, and worshipping the glorious Son of God.

The fourfold message of the church to the world should be to reject evil and be set free, to acknowledge sin and be forgiven, to give up everything and start being led, and to die and be born again into eternal life.

The church's message to the world

die and be born again

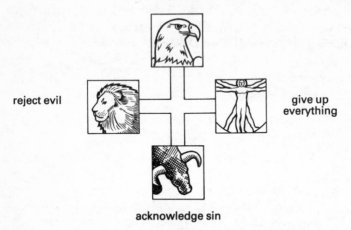

reject evil

give up
everything

acknowledge sin

It is obviously difficult for every evangelistic sermon to contain all these emphases, but over a period of time all four views should be proclaimed. Those churches and people that naturally favour one view would do well to align themselves in mission with other churches and people who can complement their own evangelism by stressing the other three aspects of the gospel, for the world needs to see and hear, not an incomplete message, but a proclamation of the full gospel.

10

Fourfold Discipleship

A brand-new fourfold relationship should begin whenever a new believer comes to Jesus and starts to trust in him. Ideally, every new convert's most earnest desire should be to make Jesus the ruler of every part of their life. Believers who know that he is the ideal ruler whom everyone needs and that his laws are perfect, will probably begin to search God's word regularly in order to grasp the principles on which to run their lives.

Hopefully, all new converts are soon taught that salvation is a pure gift from God and that sinners can never atone for their guilt. Converts who grasp this fact quickly abandon all efforts to make amends for their past sins or deficiencies. They also realise that their new relationship with their Saviour is based only on the grace and love he shows towards people who can never earn or deserve his favour. This does not mean that converts can become careless about sin. On the contrary, out of sheer gratitude they should determine to be finished with sin. But at least when they do sin, they know that they have 'an advocate with the Father, Jesus Christ, the upright' who is the sacrifice that pays the penalty for their sin (1Jn 2:1–2).

Converts today are fortunate if they are encouraged to start developing an intimate personal relationship with their new Friend, who has been tempted in every way they are without giving in to sin. Those who nurture this friendship soon discover that Jesus sympathises with all their experiences because he has, in principle, been through them all himself.

153

And all new converts should be urged to begin worshipping God, not a god of their imagination, but the God who is the truth, the source of all life, light and love.

Yet, sadly, many new believers are not helped as they should be, and never go on in their relationship with Jesus to experience the joy of God-directed, obedient living. Others are never taught that all their sins—past, present and future—have been eternally atoned for on the cross. Still more are never encouraged to know Jesus personally as an intimate, human companion. And some sing psalms, hymns or spiritual songs, but never know what it is like to be lost in wonder, love and praise in the presence of the Son of God.

These impoverished believers are greatly loved by God, and he will surely make up to them in eternity for what they have missed in life. But, for now, God expects those who know his four faces to lead others into the dazzling light of the kingdom and into the glorious life of liberty that belongs by right to all his sons and daughters.

First steps in discipleship

Jesus' first followers were called 'disciples', and the famous twelve apostles were chosen from a much larger group of ordinary disciples. All Jesus' followers today should also be encouraged to consider themselves as 'disciples', and should be urged towards a disciple's fourfold life, or biblical discipleship. As we have seen, most Christian traditions major on one or other of these basic steps of discipleship: it is better to take all four equally.

One step of discipleship is disciplined obedience. The gospel requires disciples to obey the Father, and this is only possible when they have got to know his thinking. This means careful study of the whole Bible so that a deeper and deeper understanding may be gained of the principles by which God wants his disciples to live. Jesus said that he had come to fulfil the law, not to abolish it; and the Old Testament law, supplemented and interpreted by the New Testament commandments, gives the basic guidelines for all contemporary decision-making. Christians who have grasped the important concept of justification by grace sometimes forget that, out of thankfulness, they are required to obey God and to be an exposition of the law in action.

Another step is the end of self-justification. This means that disciples admit to God, to each other, and to themselves, that they are grievous sinners whose only hope is to trust Jesus totally as their Saviour from the wrath of God. Disciples do not go about trying to justify themselves, or seeking to make up for their sins by good behaviour, religious devotion, or obedience to God's commandments. Real disciples keep the law in gratitude for the gift of forgiveness that they have already unwrapped, not in a vain attempt to earn forgiveness.

Basic discipleship

learn to worship

begin disciplined obedience

walk in the Spirit

stop justifying self

A third step is learning to walk in the Spirit. Disciples are meant to learn from the Holy Spirit how to apply the principles of God's word to today's decisions; they are meant to allow the Spirit to live his life through them and to make them more and more like Jesus. True disciples do not try harder in their own strength to be good, for that is a waste of time—if they succeeded they could become proud, and if they failed they might get depressed. Instead, true disciples consciously depend on the Spirit to do good through them. They allow him to develop his fruit in their lives, and they gradually grow towards perfection as a result of their absolute reliance on him.

The other step of discipleship is learning to worship. Disciples need to learn to express their love for God, not only by singing songs in church or receiving the Eucharist, but also by developing their talents and by doing everything—whether mundane chores or skilled work—to the very best of their ability and then offering it as a fragrant offering to God. Disciples need to create spaces and silences in their lives when they can expose themselves to God in worship, so that they can shine with his light—and not with their own—in the world.

Disciples are like the moon, which is quite dead by itself but shines in the darkness with the reflected light of the sun. The moon is eclipsed when the earth gets wholly or partly between the sun and the moon; and there is spiritual darkness in the church when the world gets between the Son of God and his disciples. However, the sun is eclipsed when the moon gets between the sun and the earth; and there is a similar spiritual darkness on earth when disciples take the limelight and hinder the passage of light from the Son of God into the world, drawing attention to themselves instead of reflecting his glory.

Submitted to God

One of the most striking features of Jesus' life is his submission to the Father; and this submission is a secret of his authority over demonic powers and the forces of nature. His submission is seen in every Gospel and throughout the New Testament, for example, 'Nevertheless, let it be as you, not I, would have it' (Mt 26:39), and, 'When everything has been subjected to him, then the Son himself will be subjected to the One who has subjected everything to him' (1 Cor 15:28). Similarly, those disciples who want to exercise the same authority as Jesus must first learn to put themselves under God's authority: they must be what Jesus was, to do what he did.

Divine submission means

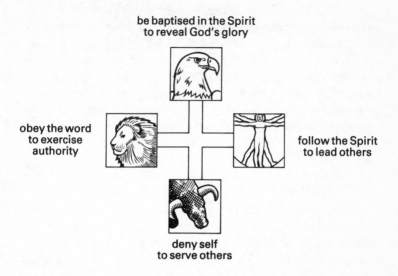

be baptised in the Spirit
to reveal God's glory

obey the word
to exercise
authority

follow the Spirit
to lead others

deny self
to serve others

A similar principle applies to service. Jesus was wholly dedicated to doing the will of his Father by serving the people among whom he had been placed and to whom he had been sent. And it was in doing this that he received all the resources of God that were necessary for his mission. It is exactly the same today: disciples who want to serve as Jesus served must submit to God's will as it is expressed in their geographical and sociological setting. First, they must serve the people around them, and then they must serve the ones to whom they are clearly sent by God. It is a principle of serving with Jesus that there will be no disciple's crown without a disciple's cross. The greater the love-inspired self-denial now, the greater the reward in heaven.

The New Testament shows that Jesus was an effective leader of men and women; he called people to follow him, and they willingly obeyed. Jesus' submission to the Holy Spirit was one secret of his leadership of others. And the same is true for his followers today: those disciples who want to be effective leaders or outstanding examples must first learn to listen to and follow the promptings of the Spirit.

The Gospels show that Jesus received the Holy Spirit before doing the great miracles that revealed his glory, and that after receiving the Spirit and before beginning his ministry, he prayed and waited in the desert. The apostles had the Spirit breathed upon them by Jesus, but then they had to wait in Jerusalem until they were filled with power from on high. And any modern-day disciples who want to share God's life and radiate his glory must also submit themselves to God's pattern of receiving his Spirit and patiently waiting for God's right time.

Submitted to people

Jesus' submission to other people is, perhaps, the most unexpected feature of his life. In demonstrating the kingdom of heaven, Jesus showed his disciples what it means to be a citizen of earth. So he meekly submitted to his parents, to his cousin John, to the weekly worship at the synagogue, to the Roman and Jewish authorities in the payment of taxes, to the Jewish high priests, to Pilate, and to the nails of the cross. And, as a man, it was in putting himself under human authorities in this way that he gained the right to exercise authority himself. Disciples who want to live and minister with Jesus' authority need to live as he lived, voluntarily under the authority of other people.

Jesus also depended on other people. He depended on his parents, on John, and on the angels who looked after him in the desert. He accepted the service of women who accompanied him on his journeys. He stayed with people who wanted to look after him. He valued the friendship and companionship of the disciples—especially the inner three. And he needed Simon of Cyrene to carry his cross for him. Jesus' dependence on other people, and on the Father, reveals a fundamental principle of all Christian service. Those disciples who want to give must be willing to receive, those who want to minister must be able to accept help, and those who want to serve must depend at all times on other people for the support and resources they need.

Human submission means

receive truth and light through others
before offering it to others

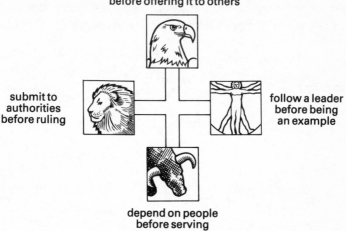

submit to
authorities
before ruling

follow a leader
before being
an example

depend on people
before serving

This principle is also true for the other sides of discipleship. Disciples cannot become effective leaders of people until they have first learned to follow men and women. Apostles—those who are sent—must always remain disciples—those who go on learning and following. And disciples cannot offer God's life, truth, love and light to the world unless they have first received it through other Christian people. God pours his love into a disciple's life by the Holy Spirit, but he usually involves a human intermediary in the process: disciples need to learn to receive God's truth and light from other disciples if they are to pass them on effectively.

Anointed with the Spirit

Jesus did not submit himself to God and to other people just for the sake of submitting. Instead, he submitted so that he could exercise authority, serve sacrificially, lead with perfection, and display God's glory. But submission alone was not enough to achieve these goals; Jesus had to be anointed with the Holy Spirit as well. It is still the same for disciples today. The anointing with, or baptism in, the Holy Spirit is given to enable submitting disciples to live with the effectiveness of Jesus—though none manage to live consistently as people filled with the Spirit.

The Spirit is given as

power
to display glory

power
to defeat evil

power
to move towards
a perfect life

power
to serve sacrificially

God immerses his disciples in the Spirit to equip them to exercise his authority over all evil powers. Many Western Christians still deny or ignore the reality of demons, though few Christians living in the Third World can do so. But the serious growth of witchcraft and satanism, and the pastoral experiences of those who are trying to help people who are unmistakably possessed, tell the same story as the New Testament: exorcism is sometimes necessary, and it can be achieved in the authority of the name of Jesus and in the power of the Holy Spirit, for all who are prepared to renounce their involvement in evil practices and turn to Jesus.

Secondly, the baptism in the Spirit introduces disciples to a life of service following the example of Jesus' life. This includes authority to heal in his name, but the most important and neglected aspect is the ability to sacrifice oneself for others, to lay down one's life in the service of believers and unbelievers alike. When Jesus was anointed with the Spirit at his baptism, God did two things which underline the vital link between sacrificial service and the Spirit. He inspired John to introduce Jesus as Lamb of God, and he sent the Spirit in the shape of a dove. The Lamb implied that Jesus was to be the greatest sufferer of all time. And the dove pointed to Jonah (the name means dove), whose service involved great suffering, and to sacrifice, for the dove was an alternative offering for Jews who could not afford a lamb or a goat. There would be less pride in some congregations if the relationship between the Spirit and truly sacrificial living were more fully understood.

Thirdly, the anointing with the Spirit is given to help disciples live a life which is moving towards perfection; and to enable them to understand other people with the understanding and sympathy of Christ. The Spirit is the *parakletos*, the one who is called alongside, so he calls disciples to get close to those with whom they have little in common, or even profoundly disagree. He is the 'Counsellor', so any anointing with the Spirit is bound to help disciples bring God's counsel to people. And he is the 'Comforter', so he naturally helps disciples to comfort and encourage people, even those whom they do not especially like.

And the Spirit is given to enable disciples to radiate God's love, to shine with his light and truth, to display more and more of his glory—making God's presence felt in deeply practical ways. As with all the foursomes in this book, there is overlap; but if each aspect of the Spirit does not have its place, a disciple's experience will be unbalanced, and other people will get an inaccurate impression of God's great gift of the Holy Spirit to his believing children.

The Spirit-filled life

The fourfold principle occasionally emerges in Paul's writings. For example, in 2 Timothy 1:7 he reminds his protégé of four characteristics which should be seen in the Spirit-filled disciple's life: 'God did not give us a spirit of timidity, but the Spirit of power and love and self-control.'

The Spirit brings

love

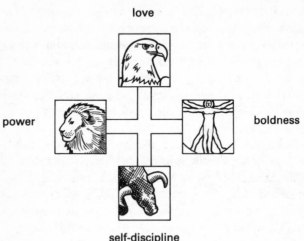

power

boldness

self-discipline

Disciples should not be timid. When Jesus was arrested his disciples forsook him and fled, but after Pentecost a great change took place. No matter how much they were flogged or imprisoned, the disciples never stopped teaching and proclaiming the good news about Jesus. Many disciples today are either shy and reserved, or feel that their Christian experience is a private matter. But when those same disciples are filled with the Holy Spirit, whether or not this happens, as it did for Timothy, through the laying on of hands, they usually find that they want to tell their friends what Jesus has done for them, and that they can overcome their natural timidity and embarrassment.

Disciples should also be filled with power. The Greek word is *dunamis,* from which the word 'dynamite' is derived. It describes God's power to defeat Satan and dismiss him from any situation, to stand in the face of ridicule and persecution, to overcome fear and speak about Jesus, and to do the mighty works which Jesus did when he was on earth. This power is not derived from natural enthusiasm or strength of character; it comes from the all-powerful Holy Spirit.

Disciples should be full of love. When the Spirit comes, disciples begin to love God as they have never loved him before. They find that their hearts are enlarged towards other Christians, even those with different temperaments and theologies, and towards the masses who are not yet part of his family. Again, this is not natural human love, it is God's love which is poured into disciples' hearts by the Holy Spirit. It is the kind of love that goes on loving however discouraging the response or reaction.

And Spirit-filled disciples should also be characterised by self-control or self-discipline, a mark of the servant spirit who enables disciples to deny self in the service of God and man. Paul supremely showed all these four qualities of discipleship in his missionary service and in his many sufferings for the gospel, and he attributed them all to the work of God's Spirit in his life.

Sacrificial discipleship

God is always calling all his disciples to a more definite discipleship, and this involves sacrifice. Every aspect of a disciple's Christian life should have both a passive and an active element, for they must receive before they can give, and they must be broken before Jesus can work effectively through them. Jesus made it plain that without real sacrifice there will never be real effectiveness: 'If anyone wants to be a follower of mine, let him renounce himself and take up his cross every day and follow me' (Lk 9:23).

So God calls his subjects to sacrifice their proud self-will, to learn to obey and to submit in order that Jesus may exercise his heavenly authority through them. He orders his subjects to obey the commands in his word so that they can live in the world by the authority of his word. He orders them to obey the promptings of his Spirit so that they can rule over evil in the power of the Spirit. He orders them to submit to one another in his church so that they can exercise his authority in the church. And he orders his subjects to submit to the structures of society so that they can establish his kingdom on earth.

God calls his disciples to

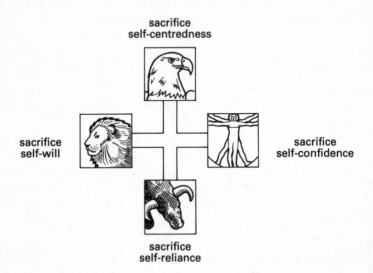

sacrifice
self-centredness

sacrifice
self-will

sacrifice
self-confidence

sacrifice
self-reliance

God calls his servants to sacrifice their proud self-reliance, to learn to depend and to accept help in order that Jesus may serve more effectively through them. He tells his servants to depend on the promises of his word so that they can serve in the world according to the demanding standards of the word. He tells them to depend on the leading of the Spirit so that they can serve the needy in the power of the Spirit. He tells them to depend on his help through other people so that they can serve one another in the church. And he tells his servants to depend on the society in which he has placed them so that they can serve the community around them.

God calls his friends to sacrifice their proud self-confidence, to learn to follow an example in order that Jesus may use their lives as an example to inspire others. He asks his friends to dedicate themselves to following his example in the word so that they can

demonstrate what Jesus is like to the world. He asks them to welcome his encouragements from the Spirit so they can encourage
others to be like him. He asks them to welcome his correction and
encouragement through one another in the church so that they
can bear with one another in the church. And he asks his friends
to welcome everything that is good in society so that they can
show his standards and approval in their community.

And God also calls his children to sacrifice their proud self-centredness, to learn to worship and to accept eternal life in order
that they may demonstrate God's eternal nature. He longs for his
children to receive Jesus as the Son of God who is revealed in the
word so that they can proclaim his eternal truth to the world. He
longs for them to receive the anointing of the Spirit so that they
can shine with his eternal light in earth's dark places. He longs for
them to receive his love through one another in the church so that
they can enjoy his divine love with each other in the church. And
he longs for his children to receive insights about the nature of life
from his glorious creation, so that they can care with his love for
every aspect of his creation.

United in the church

Whenever a new believer comes to Jesus and begins to trust in
him, a brand-new relationship starts, not only with God but also
with all other Christians in the church. Paul shows that Jesus'
death united Jews and Gentiles, making one entity out of the two,
and that his purpose in this was 'to create a single New Man out
of the two of them, and through the cross, to reconcile them both
to God in one Body' (Eph 2:15–16). This means that although
every individual disciple undoubtedly has a personal relationship
with God, they are also all united with each other and with God.

Peter gives a 'foursome' which describes the marvellous unified
calling of disciples: 'You are a chosen people, a royal priesthood,
a holy nation, a people belonging to God, that you may declare
the praises of him who called you out of darkness into his wonderful light' (1 Pet 2:9, NIV). Peter's descriptions express the same
basic ideas as Paul's four terms for united disciples—a bride

(2 Cor 11:2), a holy temple (1 Cor 3:16), a body (Eph 1:23) and the church (1 Cor 1:2).

United disciples are

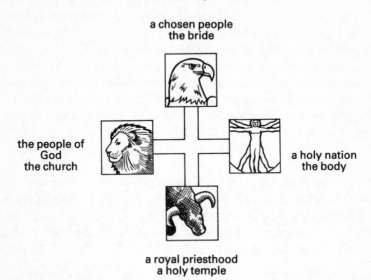

a chosen people
the bride

the people of
God
the church

a holy nation
the body

a royal priesthood
a holy temple

Disciples are the people who have been carefully chosen from all other people to be the beloved bride of the Son of God. God really has chosen them. His word cannot be broken. His love never fails. And the bride will share his Son's inheritance of all that there is. These are breathtaking thoughts beyond all imagining, yet they are the simple truth. Disciples are loved with an eternal love, and:

> ... neither death nor life, nor angels, nor principalities, nothing already in existence and nothing still to come, nor any power, not the heights nor the depths, nor any created thing whatever, will be able to come between us and the love of God, known to us in Christ Jesus our Lord (Rom 8:38–39).

Peter was writing to disciples who were facing severe persecution, to people who were likely to be asked to serve Jesus by laying down their lives. So he calls them a royal priesthood, that is, they serve the king by sacrificially serving the king's people in all sorts of ways, and by filling themselves, his holy temple, with the priestly sacrifices of praise, prayer and thanksgiving. In any country with a monarchy it is considered a very high privilege to serve the royal family in their royal palace; so it must be an incalculable honour to wear the uniform of those signed with the cross, and to serve the King of kings—even if it does sometimes mean martyrdom.

The unified disciples are also, according to Peter, a holy nation. This means that they have been set apart for a corporate life of dedication and consecration, as was the Son of Man. Paul's favourite term is the body: disciples are formed into the body of the Son of Man so that he can carry on living his perfect life on earth through them.

And they are a people who belong to God: they are his church (the Greek word *ekklesia* means gathering), citizens of his heaven and children of his kingdom. They are subject to God's laws and directed by God's Spirit. They are the Lord's.

Prepared for service

Paul shows that the leadership structure of the church, perhaps not surprisingly, reflects the fourfold principle. He states that the ascended Jesus gave gifts to humanity, and that 'to some, his "gift" was that they should be apostles; to some prophets; to some, evangelists; to some, pastors and teachers; to knit God's holy people together for the work of service to build up the body of Christ' (Eph 4:11–12).

It is sad that many local congregations have read this scripture for so long, and yet have expected their minister to be omnicompetent and fulfil all the leadership roles. And it is even sadder that church leaders have studied it and yet ignored its implications for their situation. The Head of the church does not give every gift to one individual, for he wants all his disciples to depend on each other. He has ordained that there should be four main leadership roles in his church, and these reflect the four faces of God.

Ministries for the church

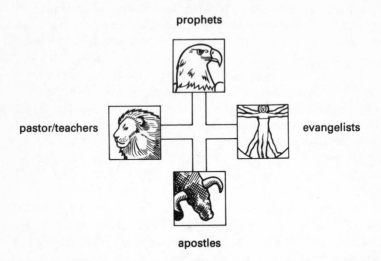

The word 'apostle' means 'one who is sent'. The first apostles were sent ahead of Jesus to the places he would be visiting, and true apostles are always pioneers who are sent ahead to spearhead the work of the gospel. Their role is to demonstrate the presence of God by their actions as well as their preaching; by their patient and sacrificial service, they earn the right of the church to be heard. Apostles may be unpopular, many of them have had to lay down their lives, but they are the people who establish new Christian communities. Filled, as they should be, by the spirit of active self-sacrifice, they represent the serving face of God.

Prophets have always been called to live in very close communion with God. They enter into his presence to hear his thoughts, and they emerge to preach, to encourage, to explain what God is doing, or to challenge the standards and behaviour of the church and the world. Ideally, they only pass on what God is thinking and doing, and do not taint the message with their own opinions, attitudes and cultural values. By temperament and calling they are closest to the divine face of God.

Evangelists are not so much the Billy Grahams of the church (people like him are either apostles or prophets), rather, they are the many church members whose special gifts are living the ordinary, dedicated life of the human face of God, and gossiping the good news in language that the people with whom they live and work understand.

Pastor/teachers build on the foundations which are laid by the other three types of leaders. They stay in one place, often for many years, caring for the church, teaching it the word of God and the ways of Jesus, establishing the kingdom on sure and lasting scriptural foundations, and emphasising its essential unity with all Christians down the centuries, through the traditions and across the world.

Of course, the four categories are not mutually exclusive. Every disciple who is filled with the Spirit of the fourfold Jesus should have something of each of his characteristics; and there are often occasions when every Christian, whatever his or her principal calling, needs to act in an apostolic, prophetic, evangelistic or pastoral manner. But the four types of leaders should be encouraged to concentrate on their particular gift, while asking God to raise up colleagues with the complementary gifts and depending on leaders from different traditions who possess other gifts. They should also be urged to share responsibilities more widely in areas where they are less gifted. If more Christians did both of these things more frequently, the church would undoubtedly grow more rapidly in both numbers and spiritual maturity.

The church's service

Paul shows in Ephesians 4:12 that the four types of leaders were given by Jesus to prepare the church for service. And the Greek word he uses, *diakonia,* means practical, menial, foot-washing service. Each individual disciple is clearly meant to serve God, other disciples and the world, but the four leaders are meant to ensure that the church as a whole is characterised by this sort of humble service.

In summary, the church has four serving functions in the world.

God wants his church to demonstrate that Jesus is the King of kings by obeying his word, acting with his authority, and relying on his name; to show that Jesus is the Saviour by depending on his death, serving with his effectiveness and relying on his blood; to make it plain that Jesus is the supreme human being by following in his footsteps, leading with his perfection and imitating his example. And God means the church to reveal that Jesus is God by receiving his life, his light, his truth and his love; by sharing his life, shining with his light, speaking his truth and showing his love; and by relying at all times on his Holy Spirit.

Discipleship will be delightful when the whole church serves like this. Perhaps, then, the whole earth really will be filled with the glory of God, as the waters cover the sea.

11

Fourfold Prayer

All disciples and all Christian congregations would be helped if they occasionally checked whether the balance of emphases seen in the four faces of God were being faithfully reproduced in the different areas of their Christian lives. However, there is one area of Christian living where it is, perhaps, more important than any other that the fourfold principle be enthusiastically followed. Prayer is the air that helps disciples to stay healthy, and all believers need to understand that every aspect of their praying and worshipping should be shaped in God's fourfold image.

Although prayers are sometimes offered either to Jesus or to the Holy Spirit, the normal New Testament pattern is for prayer to be made to the Father, through the Son, in the Spirit. Some people address all their prayers to 'Father', while others prefer to speak only to 'Lord' or 'Almighty God'. However, the Old Testament contains enough names or aspects of God's nature for a name of God to be chosen which is appropriate to the prayer being prayed. And as God has revealed himself primarily as *Yahweh Sabaoth, El Elyon, El Shaddai,* and *El Qodesh,* it is sensible to focus on these aspects of God when praying. If the prayer is for God to overcome an enemy, it is more relevant to address the powerful 'Lord of hosts' than the perfect 'Holy One'. And it makes no sense to concentrate on, say, 'the Most High' if the petition is for God to provide much needed resources when 'the Breasted God' (traditionally 'Almighty God') has been revealed throughout Scripture as the providing side of God. Of course, God is so gracious that he hears and answers his disciples' prayers whatever name is used, but when he has revealed his nature in such a rich variety of names, it seems somewhat strange for his children to ignore them.

Prayer is

purposed by the triune God

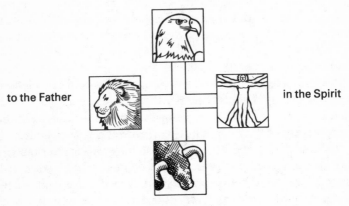

to the Father   in the Spirit

through the Son

All prayer is made possible through the Son. At his death, the four-coloured Temple curtain was torn from top to bottom, from heaven to earth, thus making it possible for all those who trust in him to enter the Holiest Place and speak to God face to face. And when they do this in prayer, Jesus personally directs his disciples so that they can pray in his name with his personal authority. He also sustains their praying by interceding on their behalf; gives them the example of his own perfect praying so that they have a pattern to follow; and offers them the life and the light which will enable them to pray more naturally in line with the Father's will.

Effective prayer is made in the strength of the Spirit. Disciples are filled with the power of the Spirit so that they can resist the natural and demonic temptations not to pray, or not to persist in praying. They are aided by the Spirit's own prayers, for when they 'do not know how to pray properly' the Spirit personally makes their petitions for them 'in groans that cannot be put into words' (Rom 8:26). They are filled or anointed with the *parakletos*, who quietly encourages them to pray, and then counsels and advises them on what to pray. And they are immersed or baptised in the Holy Spirit to ensure that their prayers are motivated only by God's divine love and a desire to glorify his holy name.

All prayers offered by disciples are purposed by the Trinity. From the human level, believers appear to be caught up in a haphazard spiritual struggle. Their prayers ebb and flow in response to their mood, their commitment, their circumstances, and the strength of the opposition. Sometimes they pray with fervour and power, while at other times they are lukewarm and apathetic—often there appears to be no pattern or purpose to their praying. But from the divine viewpoint every believer is prayerfully involved in a carefully planned battle; and the triune God has allocated their prayers a limited, but clearly defined, role in the war. After the triune God has together established the strategy, the different Persons of the Godhead carry out their respective functions perfectly, and the praying members of the church perform their limited functions to the best of their obedience and resources.

The disciples' role in prayer

Whenever disciples pray, they have four roles. They pray as citizens of the kingdom of heaven who are under the authority of the King of kings, and as liberators who are triumphing in Jesus' name. Because Jesus is the rightful ruler of every situation that is brought to God in prayer, all praying disciples can pray authoritatively—especially with regard to Satan and the forces of evil.

However, they also pray as sick people who have been made whole, as sinners who have been justified, and as servants who know they can pray only because they are supported by the constant intercession of Jesus their great High Priest. There are many times when disciples need to be healed before they can offer healing, need forgiveness before they can hear a confession, and need to be prayed for so that they can pray for others. Therefore all disciples should pray with humility—especially when they are interceding for the sick.

Disciples pray as

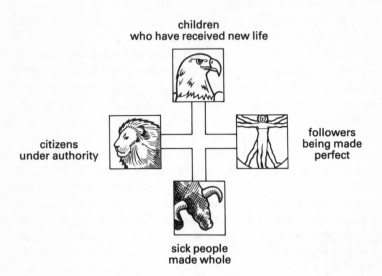

children
who have received new life

citizens
under authority

followers
being made
perfect

sick people
made whole

Disciples also pray as followers of Jesus who are being made perfect by his spotless humanity, and as examples to others because they are indwelt by his Holy Spirit. When disciples really are following the example of Jesus and the prompting of the *parakletos*, they will pray with the compassion, concern and tears of Jesus, and will become more and more like Jesus in his ability to be alongside people. So they should pray with sympathy and understanding—especially for the ordinary problems of life.

And they pray as believers who are the fruit of Jesus' labour, as people who have received his heavenly life and light, and as demonstrators of his love and truth. Everybody picks up some sort of likeness from their parents; disciples are meant to spend so much time in their Father's presence that they pick up many of his mannerisms. In consequence, their fourth role in prayer is to speak with his holiness, to shine with his glory, and to show something of his mystery.

The concerns of prayer

When the fourfold principle is applied to prayer, it helps to correct believers' imbalances, to reduce the effects of their prejudices, and to broaden their limited horizons.

The kingdom should be one concern of prayer. Disciples regularly pray 'your kingdom come, your will be done on earth as it is in heaven'. So they should be praying for Jesus to rule every part of their lives, and for more people to obey him in their congregation and nation. There is an element of warfare in the prayer, 'deliver us from the Evil One'; and believers should go on to pray against all the devices of the devil, and claim the victory of Jesus in situations that are not as they should be.

Service should be another concern. Disciples often pray 'forgive us our sins', and this should lead on to fervent prayer for God to meet all the needs of the sinful, the sick, the mentally ill, the homeless, the needy, the exasperating, the unpleasant and so on. But they also go on to pray 'as we forgive those who sin against us', so the prayers of disciples should always lead on to effective action. To pray is not to pass the complete responsibility to God. Instead, to pray is to ask God to meet the needs that disciples cannot meet themselves, and to ask him to strengthen disciples to serve the needs that they have been given the resources to meet.

The ordinary human problems of life should be a third concern of prayer. Modern-day disciples in Western Europe pray 'give us this day our daily bread', even when their freezers and cupboards are overflowing with food. It might be better if they prayed instead for the problems that really concerned people—debt, social and family disintegration, unemployment and civil unrest. They should also pray that they themselves become more like Jesus, and that their friends and fellow-disciples increase in understanding, sympathy, patience, friendliness and joy.

The concerns of prayer

God

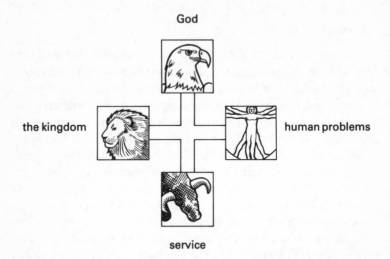

the kingdom   human problems

service

A fourth concern is God himself. The Lord's Prayer begins with the words, 'Our Father in heaven, hallowed be your name', and disciples should be concerned to honour God in their prayers. They should spend time worshipping and love God for his sake, not theirs. They should honestly want their public and private prayers to be answered so that his name might be honoured, and not for their own gratification. They should be concerned to give God reason to be proud of his children, and Jesus reason to be delighted with his bride. They should be worried that some Christians appear not to be baptised in the Spirit, while others do not seem to be living in the fullness of his power. And their prayers should reflect God's distress at the apathy of so many towards their Creator and Redeemer, and at the blasphemy in some religions around the world.

It is easy for any disciple to slip into the habit of praying for only one or two of these areas of concern, but the four concerns should each have their proper place in individual and congregational prayer, just as in the Lord's pattern prayer.

The divine content of prayer

A disciple's prayer-life will be even more balanced when the four-fold principle is also applied to the divine and human content of their praying.

Disciples often call Jesus 'Lord', but this is only real if they are putting the whole of their lives under his direction. But if he is 'Lord', they need to know his will, and this involves hard, persistent study of God's thinking as it is outlined in the Scriptures. This cannot be achieved with a quick reading of Bible reading notes, but only by setting aside real time to studying the word and attempting to grasp the whole counsel of God. There is no short cut to knowing the mind and wisdom of God.

Then, as disciples begin to understand God's thinking, they need to apply it day by day, thinking God's way, living under his authority, never forgetting that one day they will have to give an account of their lives to the Judge of the whole earth. They also need to be thankful because the king has given them so much, and because Paul commands, 'For all things give thanks; this is the will of God for you in Christ Jesus' (1 Thess 5:18).

Serious students of the Bible are often tempted to become more involved with theory than reality, so their study needs to be balanced by the simple spiritual disciplines of meditation and memorisation. Virtually all believers can learn the key verses which are central to the Christian faith. They can also memorise hymns and choruses without much effort, and these can help them to assimilate important matters of doctrine. And everybody can begin to meditate on the promises in God's word, on Jesus' parables, and on the beauty of God's creation: it is by meditating that the truths of Scripture and creation are drawn into the human spirit, and are then digested and experienced.

Many Christians find it helpful to have a small cross or crucifix in front of them when they pray or read God's word. They do not use such an object as a charm, or worship it as a graven image; instead they look to it as a visual reminder of God's great sacrifice by his suffering servant. Study and meditation can, on their own, tempt a disciple to start being too introspective or self-sufficient.

These disciplines need to be counterbalanced by a conscious dependence on the cross. At some stage in their praying, all disciples need to survey the cross, hate their sinfulness, confess their sins and pour contempt on all their pride.

And every Christian should spend some time in worship, praising God for who he is, celebrating his holiness, loving his beauty, and revelling in the depths of his nature. Disciples need to learn to use their God-given skills creatively to express their adoration and worship in words, songs, dance, poetry, art, needlework, carpentry, calligraphy, horticulture, flower-arranging, catering, banner-making and every conceivable art form.

The divine content of prayer

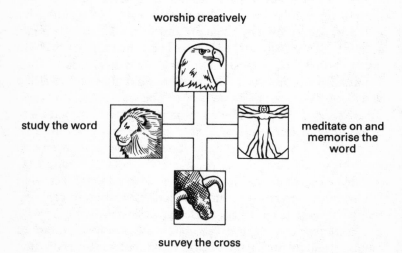

worship creatively

study the word

meditate on and memorise the word

survey the cross

The human content of prayer

Although all prayer is Godward in direction, most prayers are for people. And, again, the fourfold principle can help to bring balance to a disciple's intercessions.

All people have an enemy, and one of the disciple's roles in prayer is to free the bound. On the cross, Jesus broke in principle the power of Satan over all humanity and in every situation; but it remains for his subjects to claim and apply that victory. This is done in prayer. Some people are plainly in the grip of evil, for example those who are bound to alcohol, drugs or materialism, and with these, fasting sometimes needs to be added to prayer.

However, there are many other situations, even in the lives of Christians, where the devil is obviously at work. Sometimes prayer needs to be made to enable a friend to overcome persecution or anxiety, or to resist acute temptation, or to choose God's uprightness. In prayer, disciples announce the victory of Jesus, speak words of resistance to the devil, and command him to be removed from the situation.

Every believer knows ways in which their Christian friends and acquaintances are less than perfect. Jesus does not spend his time criticising them, either in thought or word; and neither should disciples. Instead, Jesus 'lives for ever to intercede for them' (Heb 7:25). When disciples are tempted to criticise their friends, they should join their intercessions to those of Jesus and pray for them instead. In prayer, disciples beg the Holy Spirit in some unspecified way to convict a person of a particular sin, and they urge Jesus to overwhelm that person with the awareness that this sin is adding to the Father's sadness and the supreme cost of the cross.

And every believer knows people who need some sort of healing, whether physical or emotional. There are people with fevers, and those who easily get het up. There are some people who are paralysed, and there are others who insist that they cannot do anything. A few people have leprosy, but many more think that they are a terrible sight. Occasionally someone has a withered hand, but people often feel that they cannot do one particular task. Some people are blind, whereas others feel that they are groping in the dark. Many people are deaf, and even more are convinced that they cannot hear God's voice in the way that others do. A few people are lame, and some just limp along in their spiritual lives. One or two people are dumb, but large numbers of people insist that they cannot praise God as others do. And serving Jesus can heal them all.

So believers bring them to Jesus in prayer, and beg, and beg, and beg, and go on begging until the person is healed.

> I tell you, if the man does not get up and give it him for friendship's sake, persistence will make him get up and give his friend all he wants. So I say to you: Ask, and it will be given to you; search, and you will find; knock and the door will be opened to you (Lk 11:8–10).

The human content of prayer

care for God's honour

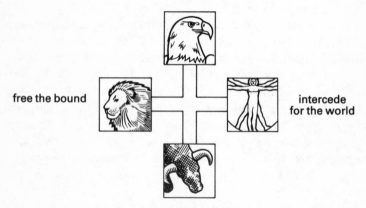

free the bound

intercede for the world

convict and heal the church

All disciples have a Friend who cares deeply about all the sorrows and hurts and deprivations of fallen humanity, both generally throughout the world, and particularly in the lives of all the people known to that disciple. When a man or woman gets close to a friend they inevitably start to share that friend's interests and concerns. So as disciples draw closer and closer to Jesus, they should find themselves starting to pray about the human concerns of Jesus.

They pray for the starving in Africa, and for the man down the road whose right knee is giving him pain. They pray for the Third

World nations crippled by unjust debt, and for their neighbours' difficult marriage. They pray for political prisoners the world over, and for the woman in the next village whose husband is in prison for theft. They pray for the Western nations who are infatuated with material possessions, and for their grandchild who is about to start school. They pray for the millions who worship other gods, and for more consecration in their own small chapel. And, knowing that *El Shaddai* is well capable of attending to the needs of 5,000 million people at once, they confidently leave all these matters with him.

And then they remember the fourfold principle, and realise that God should be honoured in the lives of the people for whom they have prayed. So they pray that their worship might be sincere and without wandering thoughts; that their love for God and his people may increase beyond bounds; that they may be filled more and more with his wonderful Spirit, and become more and more like him in character and deed. They pray that, like the Son, they may live with the Father and give him the glory in all that they do. They cry out to Jesus to come again soon. And then they end their prayers with an exhausted 'Amen'.

12

Conclusion

In Part One we tried to answer the two questions, 'Why are there four Gospels, and not six or three?'; and, 'Why did God allow the differences between these Gospels to exist?' Throughout the book we have sought to demonstrate the general principle (not the fixed rule) that there are four Gospels because it has always pleased the Holy Spirit to reveal the essence of God's nature in four main sides or faces of God.

In answering the two questions it has been possible in Part Two to suggest a balanced view of what the Christian life is all about. The fourfold principle shows that it has reference to Satan—that he should be comprehensively defeated; to others—that they should be served and cared for; to ourselves—that we should be becoming perfect; and to God—that he should be given all the honour.

In each case, Jesus has done his part to perfection. The woman's offspring has crushed the serpent's head (Gen 3:15); and our part is to apply that victory in our lives and in the lives of others. The suffering servant of God, the Saviour of the world, the healer of humanity, has borne our sin, carried our sorrows, and accepted our punishment (Is 53:4–5). Our part is to accept that wonderful sacrifice, to trust in it for our final health in body, mind and spirit, and to offer it on his behalf to all humankind. The Christ, the anointed perfect man, has left us an example so that we can walk in his steps (1 Pet 2:21). Our part is to follow that example, to live a life of complete consecration, and to let his indwelling Spirit deal with all our human weaknesses. And the glorious Son of God has planted the seed of the tree of eternal life and has strained for our heavenly birth. So with new eyes we can see his glory, with new lips we can praise him, and with new wonder we can see ourselves as chosen by him to share his life for all eternity.

We have seen that there are four main names of God, four different colours in the Tabernacle, four bloody offerings, four great reasons why Jesus came, four things happening at his baptism, four aspects to his mission, four accomplishments on the cross, four gifts after the ascension, and four ways of describing the unified church. And we can now look at Jesus in four main ways, discover that he expects four principal responses from us, and see four sides to many of our activities as disciples.

The list of scriptural examples of the fourfold principle is seemingly endless, and to think about them and to compile our own list of foursomes is of great practical value. This book has given a few clues on where to begin, and great spiritual rewards await those who are prepared to allow the Spirit to take them deeper into these truths about the four faces of God and the fourfold nature of Jesus.

Practical consequences

Those of us in East Sussex who have spent many years studying these insights have found that, not surprisingly, they have done four main things for us.

First, they have shown us the unity of the people of God. We have slowly come to realise that most of the differences between the denominations and traditions have sprung from an overemphasis on one aspect of truth. And we have had to learn that just as one Gospel writer could never reveal the full richness of Jesus, so one believer, one congregation, one tradition, can never faithfully reveal the fullness of Christ and his gospel. Matthew's Gospel, for example, could not stand alone, it had to be placed next to Mark's, Luke's and John's. But the four all retain their special emphases and distinctions. So, too, we need to celebrate and appreciate the differences between churches and their traditions, while standing next to each other in worship and witness because we know that the fourfold Jesus can only be seen when we do. 'May they be so perfected in unity that the world will recognise that it was you who sent me' (Jn 17:23).

Practical consequences

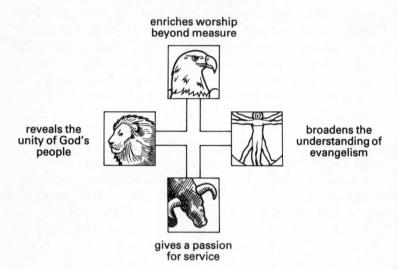

enriches worship
beyond measure

reveals the
unity of God's
people

broadens the
understanding of
evangelism

gives a passion
for service

Secondly, the insights have given us a passion for service, and a real sense of urgency as we have come to see the full extent of what has been entrusted to the church. Many of us have come from traditions which stressed the primacy of evangelism, and we have had to grasp the complementary value of humble, menial service. Some of us overemphasised the ministry of healing for a while, but we have come to see that sacrificial service has to go hand in hand with miracles. God wants us to be as enthusiastic about washing the sick as we are to heal the sick.

Thirdly, the insights have widened our understanding of evangelism and have made plain our vital need of the Holy Spirit. We have been forced to recognise that the example of our own lives is either the strength or the weakness of our evangelism, that human friendships lead more people to Christ than powerful preaching, and that without the help of the Spirit we will be unable to reach anyone with the gospel.

And fourthly, the insights have enriched our worship beyond measure. We have begun to check regularly that we are worshipping each face of God more or less equally, and we have been inspired to celebrate his infinitely complex nature. We have tasted worship with other Christian traditions, and have been enriched by their songs, symbols, rituals and musical traditions. We have had to expand our repertoire of songs and hymns to ensure that every aspect of Jesus is fully adored. We have used a variety of other art-forms to help us to worship God more creatively. And we have tried to maintain a constant chain of prayer to give a continuous offering of prayer and praise to God.

John Bickersteth's life revolved around his fourfold Jesus. He established his home, Ashburnham Place, as a conference centre where churches from every denomination could spend a week or a weekend receiving authoritative biblical teaching. He and his wife served sacrificially in the office and kitchens, preparing meals, cleaning floors and administrating the complex. He restored the ruined stable-block as the base for a community of ordinary people who were consecrated to following Christ in their own small Sussex villages. He was Vicar of two churches and was equally at home in shirt-sleeves singing choruses or in robes chanting psalms. He knew that his God was far more interested in his heart than in his musical tastes.

John Bickersteth was an authoritative Bible teacher, but he also suffered terribly: he nearly had a nervous breakdown, he lost most of his sight in a domestic accident, he had a very weak heart, and he endured cancer for three years before he died. However, John will not be remembered by those who knew him primarily as a teacher, administrator or vicar, but as an outstanding example of what a Christian man should be.

And John was always and obviously devoted to his God. He was an apostle who had been sent to Sussex to pioneer charismatic renewal. He loved to worship God, and John was never happier than when he was singing carols outside his parishioners' homes. He was related to a long line of hymn-writing clerics, but the only hymn that he himself wrote was an attempt, when he was dying of cancer, to summarise the fourfold Jesus into just six stanzas.

This book is a small memorial to an outstanding life. But when Christian people sing the last stanza of John's only hymn, they come as close as it is possible to get to his heart. *'Fill us with your Holy Spirit'* was John's greatest prayer for his own life, for his family, and for all the people he loved in East Sussex. And I am sure that, in paradise, it is now his dearest prayer for all the good people who have read this book.

> Jesus, in your fourfold nature,
>   Largely in your world ignored,
> Judge, Redeemer, Friend, Creator,
>   King and Servant, Man and Lord.
>
> Truly Everlasting Father,
>   Rightful ruler of all things,
> Final victor over Satan,
>   Death-destroying King of kings.
>
> Saviour, healer, suffering servant,
>   Sinners' ransom-sacrifice,
> On the cross for our salvation
>   Once for all you paid the price.
>
> Christ, anointed Son of Mary,
>   Man's example, friend and guide,
> Tested in all ways as we are,
>   Bearing all our griefs you died.
>
> Source of life, light, love and glory,
>   Son of God you came to earth;
> Stretched in fearsome pain you suffered,
>   Travailed for our heavenly birth.
>
> Fill us with your Holy Spirit,
>   Come back soon and take your bride,
> So that we may live for ever,
>   Whole and perfect at your side.

EXERCISES FOR PART TWO

I hope that, as well as being read privately, this book will also be used in small groups. The following exercises can be used by readers on their own, but they will be particularly useful for groups who are studying the chapters in Part Two. I trust that these exercises will help all readers to assess how well they have grasped the principles set out in Part Two.

Chapter Seven

1 The four cups of the Jewish Passover represent the four 'I shall' promises of Exodus 6:6–7. The third cup represents the ancient promise, 'I shall redeem you with outstretched arms' (Ex 6:6), and it was while drinking this cup that Jesus instituted the Christian Eucharist or Communion.

It is obvious that this promise particularly reveals the serving face of God and all the emphases that go with it. But can the other promises be allocated to particular faces? John Bickersteth and I disagreed; what do you think?

a 'I shall free you from forced labour.'
b 'I shall rescue you from their slavery.'
c 'I shall redeem you with outstretched arms.'
d 'I shall take you as my people and I shall be your God.'

2 In what way did the Jewish Tabernacle furnishings and priestly garments point towards the Christian understanding of God as a holy Trinity?

3 Which of the four main Old Testament names of God and aspects of his character does your congregation most emphasise, and which does it most neglect?

Chapter Eight

4 Most congregations and Christians celebrate Christmas using an homogenised version of the nativity story that ignores the insight which is only seen from Mark's serving point of view. A very few Christians only celebrate Christmas from Mark's viewpoint. How could your congregation use the fourfold principle to celebrate Christmas more helpfully?

5 I have suggested that every miracle, whether in history or today, can be examined and responded to from any one of the four viewpoints, but that a balanced response is to be preferred. How could your attitude to the miraculous be brought to a better fourfold balance?

6 In your congregational worship do you focus least on Jesus as ruler, or as servant, or as companion or as God? What hymns and songs do you know that would help you to worship this particular face more?

Chapter Nine

7 What were your positive or negative reasons for becoming a Christian? How have these reasons affected your witnessing and evangelism?

8 What are the different gospel emphases of the congregations geographically nearest to you? Which congregations could complement your own congregation's emphasis to reveal the fullness of Jesus' fourfold nature?

9 In what ways could the fourfold principle be used to improve your mission and evangelism?

Chapter Ten

10 What steps of discipleship would help you to become an even more balanced and devoted disciple?

11 How can the fourfold pattern of church leadership be developed more fully in your locality?

12 What do you think God is hoping that you will sacrifice?

Chapter Eleven

13 Matthew's version of the Lord's Prayer contains seven petitions. John and I could not agree how to allocate them. To which face would you allocate each petition? And what would be the most appropriate of the four main names of God to use for each petition?

a 'Our Father in heaven, may your name be held holy.'
b 'Your kingdom come.'
c 'Your will be done, on earth as in heaven.'
d 'Give us today our daily bread.'

e 'And forgive us our debts, as we have forgiven those who are in debt to us.'

f 'And do not put us to the test.'

g 'But save us from the Evil One.'

14 Which face or aspect of prayer do you most neglect? Why?

15 How could fourfold praying be introduced to your congregation? What difference would it make to the services?

Chapter Twelve

16 What are the implications of the fourfold principle for Christian unity in your immediate locality?

17 What changes do you think God hopes will take place in your life and your congregation's life as result of your studying this book?

Scripture Index